Problems
are the
Solution

keys to
lifelong learning

Dear Dave —

Best wishes
for success
with great
questions
and thinking —
problem solving

Compiled and edited by
Steph Capra and Jenny Ryan

Capra Ryan & Associates
Brisbane, Australia

IBSN: 0-9586340-7-6

Copy Editor: Leon Capra
Cover Design: Megan Hibberd,
              Artspot, Brisbane
Printed by: Kingswood Press, Brisbane

This edition published 2002 by:
Capra Ryan & Associates
PO Box 179
CAPALABA Qld   4157
Australia

Phone: (+61) 07 3847 3961
Fax: (+61) 07 3847 1929
Email: capras@gil.com.au
Website: http://www.capraryan.com.au

Contents

Problems are the Solution

keys to lifelong learning

Contents

Problems
are the
Solution

keys to
lifelong learning

Contents

Problems
are the
Solution
keys to
lifelong learning

Contents

Problems
are the
Solution
keys to
lifelong learning

Introduction

The concept for this book came about as a result of a number of dedicated, enthusiastic teachers wanting to do more for their students – to have their students wanting to come to school, to enjoy school, to want to learn and to want to continue to learn after leaving school.

They felt that by trying what for some was a different approach; they might have more chance of reaching their students. The different approach seemed to lie in the way tasks were designed for the students – tasks designed as problems so as to provide opportunities for the development of original ideas, rather than just "reading and regurgitating" the work of others.

The concept of presenting tasks as problems is not new – many teachers have been using this model for many years, and in fact, some subject areas like Maths, Science and Technology are based on a problem-solving approach. Increasingly, Universities also are structuring courses for their students on a problem-centred basis.

In the context of this book, the term "problem" has been used rather loosely, but is intended to include the concept of a task or unit of work that is presented as a question, scenario or situation that extends beyond the fact-finding stage and has no single "right" answer. Once information relating to the topic has been gathered, the "problem" enables the student to synthesise the new information with existing prior knowledge to develop new ideas or responses to the given task.

What is problem-based learning?

Problem based learning is a curriculum design and a teaching/learning strategy. It simultaneously develops higher order thinking and disciplinary knowledge bases and skills. PBL places students in the active role of problem-solvers and confronts students with a situation that reflects the real world.

The move towards Problem-based Learning (PBL) in the curriculum has the potential to fulfil a number of educational objectives. One of the prime goals of PBL is to foster critical thinking and problem-solving skills in students. In PBL the responsibility for learning rests with the learner, rather than the teacher. PBL also allows for the integration of many concepts, which ultimately increases the relevance of what is being learned, and subsequently results in greater motivation and engagement of students.

Learning through the PBL method encourages cooperation and the development of group work. These skills have been identified as important for teamwork after graduation. Increasingly, employers too, are seeking employees with skills in problem solving and critical thinking. The main advantage of PBL is that it aims to encourage high-level cognitive processes in all students, offering a wide variety of experiences, allowing students to make choices, promoting self-management and self-evaluation.

PBL represents a philosophy towards learning rather than a specific method of teaching. Application of the PBL approach allows the focus to shift from teacher-centred activity to student-centred learning. The aim is to promote an inquiry based approach that requires students to develop and refine their problem solving skills.

In recent years, The Adelaide Declaration on National Goals for Schooling in the Twenty-First Century (1999) has given prominence to problem-based approaches to learning.

Subsequently, respective State education authorities in Australia, as well as many international education bodies have encouraged this concept through an emphasis on critical thinking, problem solving and lifelong learning in current syllabus documents.

In particular, Education Queensland has developed, and is currently trialing in selected schools, the *Productive Pedagogies* (2002) theoretical framework that enables teachers to reflect critically on their teaching practices. Considerable emphasis in this framework is placed on students using higher-order thinking operations within a problem-based curriculum.

This book brings together the work of many prominent education specialists, both here in Australia and overseas, whose work is supportive of the problem-based approach to learning and teaching.

It is exciting that so many prominent information literacy specialists have contributed articles or chapters to this book, and we would like to thank them and acknowledge the effort they have made in providing such valuable underpinnings to this work. We would especially like to thank those authors who have written specifically for this work. Their support and the contribution they have made are invaluable.

References

The Adelaide Declaration (1999) on National Goals for Schooling in the Twenty-First Century.
http://www.curriculum.edu.au/mceetya/adeldec.htm.
Accessed 11.04.02

Productive Pedagogies.
http://education.qld.gov.au/public_media/reports/curriculum-framework/productive-pedagogies/. Accessed 11.04.02

About the book and the authors:

Chapter 1: Snapshots of Information Literacy

Three articles have been selected for inclusion in this chapter to provide a range of perspectives on information literacy:

1) Problem-based Learning:
Develop Information Literacy through Real Problems.

Problem-based learning (PBL) can be a context for evaluating information and articulating ideas through argumentation. It supports critical thinking, teaching for understanding and development of student information literacy skills. The authors examine critical components of PBL in developing information literacy skills, the roles of the library media specialists, and factors facilitating and impeding the use of problem-based learning in middle schools.

Eileen E. Schroeder and E. Anne Zarinnia

Eileen E. Schroeder and E. Anne Zarinnia are Associate Professors in Educational Foundations at the University of Wisconsin-Whitewater and teach in the school library media program.

This paper was presented at Treasure Mountain 9, a Teacher-librarian think tank research retreat, which was held just before the AASL Conference, "Indianapolis and Beyond", Indianapolis, November 2001.

2) Students as Critical Thinkers: How to deal with the Info Glut.

This article offers strategies for teachers to address the issue of assisting students to manage information effectively and efficiently for the society in which they live, and to develop skills for lifelong learning. Knowledge and understanding of the process they are using will assist students to comprehend their own learning, and enable them to apply that same process to any problem-solving situation, i.e., a tool for lifelong learning.

Jenny Ryan and Steph Capra

*Steph and Jenny are co-authors, editors and publishers of this book **Problems are the Solution: Keys to Lifelong Learning**, and are the authors of the ILPO (Information Literacy Planning Overview) materials, which recently won international acclaim. This book is an extension of the workshops and professional development activities they conduct with teachers in Australia and overseas.*

3) Giant Leaps, Small Steps

The process devised at The Kings School, Parramatta, to facilitate the development of motivating developmentally appropriate student assignments is outlined in this article. Collaboration between the Head of Department or the classroom teacher and the teacher-librarian led to the evolution of a curriculum-focused, student-centred Intranet with an easily navigable interface where all assignments are published.

Megan Perry and Debbie Leatheam

Megan Perry has been the Head of Information Services at The King's School in Sydney since 1999, where she continues to be heavily involved in the debate about the integration of technology within an appropriate curriculum structure. Megan's interests include online learning, the future of school libraries and the evolving literacy debate.

Debbie Leatheam has been a teacher Librarian at The King's School Senior Library since January 2000. Debbie has an interest in online learning and the development of ICT literate students, particularly through the development of appropriate curriculum related online activities.

Chapter 2: Developing a learning culture

This article is an excerpt from the book, *Ideas of a New Millennium* by Dr Peter Ellyard (pp 77-84) published by Melbourne University Press, 1998, 2001, in which Peter describes the ingredients of a learning culture. Such a learning culture is necessary for the creation of a knowledge-based industrial structure in the 21st century and for the development of life long learning, learner driven learning individuals in Australia. The scenario outlined by Peter in this chapter describes some elements of the Education System of the Year 2010.

In *Ideas for a new millennium*, Peter describes a new emerging culture that he calls 'Planetism'. It has implications for leadership and management, for education and learning, for health and wellbeing, for industrial development, for food production and agriculture, for environmental management and for intercultural relations and understanding.

In urging the creation of an ecologically, economically, socially and culturally sustainable Planetist society in the 21st century, Peter offers a challenging vision for our own future and that of generations to come.

Peter Ellyard

Dr Peter Ellyard is a futurist and strategist who lives in Melbourne. A graduate of the University of Sydney and Cornell University, he is currently Executive Director of Preferred Futures Pty Ltd, and Chairman of the Universal Greening Group of companies and of the MyFutureFoundation. A former Executive Director of the Australian Commission for the Future, he held CEO positions in a number of public sector organisations over 15 years.

He is Adjunct Professor of Intergenerational Strategies at the University of Queensland, and a Fellow of the Australian College of Education, the Environment Institute of Australia, and the Australian Institute of Management. He has been a senior advisor to the United Nations for over twenty years.

Chapter 3: The Affective Dimension of Information Literacy

In order for students to have rewarding experiences through the information literacy process, teachers and teacher-librarians need to provide instructional guidance that is affective as well cognitive in focus. Dianne emphasises the necessity for us to understand how learners experience the information literacy process and how learning through investigation can be facilitated.

Dianne Oberg

Dianne Oberg is a Professor in teacher-librarianship in the Faculty of Education at the University of Alberta in Canada. Before coming to the University, Dianne worked as a classroom teacher and teacher-librarian in the public school system. Her research focuses on teacher-librarianship education and on the implementation and evaluation of school library programs.

Dianne's recent research includes an international study, with colleagues James Henri and Lyn Hay from Charles Sturt University, on the role of principals in developing information literate school communities.

She is also working on a Canadian study of the use of Internet in schools with a University of Alberta colleague, Dr. Susan Gibson. Dianne is the editor of an international journal, School Libraries Worldwide, and an active member of school library associations at local, national, and international levels. She is currently Chair of the Department of Elementary Education at the University of Alberta. She previously held a joint appointment with that Department and the School of Library and Information Studies

Chapter 4: Can we prevent copying? Transforming scribes into thinkers

What students learn when they gather and use information might not be what they are expected to learn. Joy argues that the outcomes expected by teachers and teacher-librarians when research papers and projects are assigned, are often not achieved, and that, for various reasons, students frequently plagiarise.

Joy McGregor

Joy McGregor, associate professor in Library and Information Studies at Texas Woman's University, teaches primarily in the area of school libraries. She came to the US from Edmonton, Alberta, Canada, where she had been a teacher and teacher-librarian. She moved to Texas after receiving her Ph.D. from Florida State University. Her research deals primarily with students' information use and effective tools for promoting information literacy.

Chapter 5: Critical literacy: a building block towards the information literate school community

In a global society endeavouring to make sense of the information surrounding us, critical literacy has proved to be a difficult concept. If we are serious about the new teaching and learning paradigm that is emerging, then critical literacy must lie in a learning culture that is informed by a conceptual understanding of information literacy.

This article supports the thesis that critical literacy, as a subset of information literacy, relies on the development of critical and creative thinking within the information process: the scaffold for continuous learning. Linda argues that the building blocks of analysis, synthesis and evaluation are the building blocks that develop critical literacy, and that critical literacy is a foundation to a sound education.

Linda Langford

Linda Langford [BEd, GCert (Gifted & Talented), MAppSci (Teacher Librarianship)] has strongly advocated, throughout her teaching career, the notion of independent and interdependent learning.

As past editor of the national journal for the Australian School Library Association, she has endeavoured to highlight issues that centre on effective teaching and learning, and the professional development of school information-services staff.

As a teacher, she has focussed on the needs of students of high intellectual potential as well as supporting initiatives in the workplace for knowledge creation and sharing. Linda is currently a PhD candidate studying knowledge systems in schools, and in particular, the dynamics of knowledge creation, sharing and use amongst teaching faculty.

Chapter 6: E-Literacies and Cybraries

This chapter is based on a previously published article: *Archive fever: Libraries and cybraries in New Times.* Journal of Adolescent and Adult Literacy, 44(5) by Dr Cushla Kapitzke.

Cushla Kapitzke presents a thought-provoking article, identifying the challenges emanating from the current transformation of traditional libraries to "cybraries". Libraries, she argues, are affected not only by technological change, but also by social and cultural change.

Given these social and political influences, there is an imperative to embrace critical information literacy that exposes students to a range of theoretical, ideological and political perspectives on current curriculum issues.

Cushla Kapitzke

Dr Cushla Kapitzke BA, MEd, Cert TchLib (BCAE), PhD (JCU)

Cushla Kapitzke has worked as a secondary teacher and teacher librarian, and is currently a lecturer in the Middle Years of Schooling program at the School of Education, The University of Queensland. Having held two Postdoctoral Research Fellowships, she has a strong research and consultancy background. Her current research interests include new technologies and multiliteracies, and the sociology of information as it relates to digital libraries and cybraries.

*Key publications include a book, **Literacy and Religion** (John Benjamins, 1995), and articles in international journals such as Journal of Adolescent & Adult Literacy, Educational Technology and Society, and Education and Information Technologies.*

Chapter 7: Facilitating problem-based learning

In his book: ***Problem-based learning: how to gain the most from PBL***, this chapter is entitled "On being a coach/facilitator". Here, Don focuses on the need for a change in attitude or a mind-shift on the part of the teacher or tutor when facilitating problem-based learning. He argues that to bring out the best in the group requires a change in role from that of lecturer or instructor to that of coach or facilitator. This then results in the need for an increased level in the development of facilitation skills on the part of the teacher.

Although writing as a lecturer of university students, the relevance of his ideas to any teacher implementing Problem-based Learning is apparent.

Donald R Woods

Dr Donald Woods is a Professor in the Department of Chemical Engineering at McMaster University, Canada.

His research interests include problem-based learning, assessment, improving student learning, developing skills in problem solving, group and team work, self-assessment, change management and life-long learning.

Dr Woods has conducted over 300 workshops on effective teaching and process skill development both in North America and abroad. He has over 400 publications including the book **"Problem-Based Learning: How to gain the most from PBL."** *Waterdown, Ont.,: D.R. Woods, 1994.*

Chapter 8: Questioning Toolkit

Questions allow us to make sense of our world. They are the most powerful tools we have for making decisions and solving problems, for inventing, changing and improving our lives as well as the lives of others.

In this chapter, Jamie offers different types of questions for us as teachers to use with our students, and explains how different questions accomplish different tasks, the features of each type of question, and how to choose appropriate questions for the task in hand.

Jamie McKenzie

Jamie McKenzie is the Editor of **From Now On – The Educational Technology Journal,** *published since 1991 at* http://fno.org, *in which he has argued extensively for information literate schools.*

Jamie has enjoyed more than 30 years working as a teacher, principal, superintendent and director of libraries, media and technology. He has now moved on to support information literacy and professional development for schools across North America.

He is internationally sought after as a speaker and authority on information literacy and has spoken extensively on the introduction of new information technologies to schools. Recently, he has paid particular attention to how information literacy may transform classrooms and schools to support student-centred, engaged learning.

Chapter 9: Assessing Learning: Points for consideration

Using a case study upon which to base his argument, James articulates the need for learning to be 'tested'. The process of assessment provides the opportunity to verify that learning has occurred, and therefore assessment is a vital and integral part of learning and teaching.

James Henri

Dr James Henri is Deputy Director of the Centre for Information Technology in School and Teacher Education, Faculty of Education, University of Hong Kong. He is also currently Vice President of IASL (International Association of School Librarianship). From 1981-2001 James held various positions at CSU including Sub Dean in the Faculty of Science and Agriculture. In 1999 he gained the ASLA Citation for outstanding contribution to teacher librarianship in Australia.

He is currently Vice President of IASL (International Association of School Librarianship)

Recent publications by J. Henri include:
Hay L, Hanson K, and Henri J (2001) *New millennium new horizons: information services in schools.* Wagga Wagga: CSTL.

Hay L and Henri J. (2000) *Enter the millennium: information services in schools.* Wagga Wagga: CSTL.

Henri J and Bonanno K (1999) *The information literate school community: best practice.* Wagga Wagga: CIS.

Hay L and Henri J (1999) *The net effect: school library media centres & the Internet.* Lanham: Scarecrow Press

Chapter 10: Problem-based tasks

These examples, shared by a number of teachers in a variety of school situations, have been included to provide a starting point for colleagues, to trigger ideas enabling the development of tasks that will motivate and engage each new group of students.

Tasks or units of work designed to provide the opportunity for students to engage in higher order-thinking skills, to problem solve, to create original thoughts and ideas are offered in this chapter under the groupings of Lower, Middle and Upper School.

Snapshots of Information Literacy

1) Problem-Based Learning: Develop Information Literacy through Real Problems

Eileen E. Schroeder and E. Anne Zarinnia

The seventh graders come as a group to the library for their annual research report. They each have a country to research and have been given a series of questions to answer on their country. The school library media specialist (SLMS) pulls relevant reference tools and shows students how to locate other materials, even creating a Web page with good country links. The students quickly rush to the computers, access the electronic encyclopedia, the *CIA World Factbook*, or other bookmarked Web sites, and have their questions answered in a period. They word-process their work, possibly even adding some pictures from the encyclopedia or the Web, and turn in polished reports.

Several days later the teacher comes in to complain that, while they look good, many of the reports sound just like encyclopedia articles. Students appear to have cut-and-pasted sections of encyclopedia articles.

The teacher asks the SLMS, "Why aren't the students critically evaluating information and using higher-level thinking skills?"

Sound familiar?

The students have been given a topic for research, had it broken into more specific questions to be answered, developed and carried out a search strategy and created a presentation from the information gathered. Isn't that what the information problem-solving process is all about? What type of thinking have we asked the students to do?

How does the following assignment differ?

A cigarette manufacturer has offered to donate a state-of-the-art computer lab to the school district. In exchange, the school is asked to allow them to place a billboard advertising their products at the edge of the school property. Should the school board accept the offer? A group of seventh and eighth-grade students take the roles of various stakeholders; local tobacco farmers, health professionals, parents and other tax-burdened community members, and school administrators looking for alternate school-funding sources. They are asked to determine the best course of action.

In their respective roles, students research the issue using print, electronic, and human sources to inform their particular perspective. They must determine what questions need to be answered, assess the information found in light of their assigned perspective, and then create a well-documented argument supporting their viewpoints. Regardless of perspective, they will be asked to come to a consensus as a group and present their conclusions with evidence to the school board.

> *These students have worked through the same information problem-solving process but with significant differences.*

They have defined the questions in greater detail and determined the most appropriate and relevant sources for information. They have located and evaluated the information found with a critical eye, selected evidence to support an argument, tested their arguments by working toward consensus as a group, and presented their solution in an authentic form.

> *Unfortunately, the first scenario is all too familiar, and the second rare.*

Students are asked by a teacher, without input from the SLMS, to carry out low-level assignments that basically require only reporting of easily located facts.

The students never have to use the information they find to solve any problem or organize it in an argument to support a thesis, but rather to just present it to an audience of one – the teacher.

> *While we preach against plagiarism, we often give assignments that encourage it and make poor use of information resources.*

The second scenario engages students in problem-solving and critical thinking through an assignment collaboratively developed by SLMSs teams of teachers.

In a joint project, the University of Wisconsin – Whitewater and local middle schools in south eastern Wisconsin are exploring problem-based learning as one instructional strategy that can help SLMSs team with teachers to develop higher-level assignments, move beyond the service role often assigned to them, and help students learn information problem-solving skills so vital in the real world. Teams of teachers and SLMSs have been collaborating over the past three years to develop and implement problem-based learning projects in various curriculum areas supported by technology.

> *Problem-based learning can be a context for developing information problem-solving skills, from defining an information need to evaluating information to articulating ideas through argumentation.*

Problem-based learning supports critical thinking, teaching for understanding and development of student information literacy skills.

Schroeder, Eileen E., & Zarinnia, E. Anne. (2001a). Problem-based learning: Develop information literacy through real problems. *Knowledge Quest*, 30(1), 34-35.

2) Students as critical thinkers: How to deal with the info glut ...

Jenny Ryan and Steph Capra

Increasingly, sophisticated technology demands that the students of today are faced with an ever-increasing deluge of information in an ever-increasing variety of formats.

> *As teachers, what strategies do we need to teach our students to survive this deluge, and to develop lifelong skills that will enable them to function well in society?*

This article is intended to provide useful classroom strategies to assist in developing students as critical users of information from pre-school to the end of primary. The skills learnt from these strategies will provide the building blocks for developing more complex and sophisticated skills during secondary schooling and at tertiary level - in fact, as an ongoing process throughout life.

The info glut

Historically, information was gathered from print sources such as books, newspapers and magazines. With the coming of the computer, and the introduction of CD-ROMs and the Internet, our approach to accessing information has been radically changed. Researchers claim that, until the Middle Ages, the human brain was capable of absorbing all the knowledge that was currently known. The invention of the printing press was the first step along a path to sharing information more widely. Then, with the advent of the Internet, the sharing of information became global.

The amount of information available increased dramatically, providing a resource almost beyond comprehension. This huge volume of information creates new problems ... how do we find our way through this maze?

More importantly however, how do we teach our students to find their way through this maze?

Students, at an increasingly young age are required to have more sophisticated skills to successfully access and use this information.

The Impact of the Information Age on Teachers and Teaching:

The computer has without doubt, been the single most significant factor in changing the way we teach and learn. With the introduction of information technology comes the need for a closer scrutiny of existing approaches to teaching students how to deal with information. It has always been crucial that students critically evaluate the appropriateness and relevance of information, from whatever source.

This is even more crucial with regard to electronic sources of information, particularly the Internet, where the volume of information is so vast and so much of the information is not relevant to the task.

> **Primarily, we as teachers need the skills to teach our students to critically select and reject from this wealth of information.**

We need to develop critical thinkers!   This emphasizes the need for ongoing professional development to acquire new teaching techniques that deal with accessing information in different formats.

Current syllabus documents reflect this trend by stipulating student outcomes relating to critical thinking, problem solving and the acquisition of skills for lifelong learning.

The Impact of the Information Age on Students and Student Learning:

It is very easy for students to feel they are drowning in the deluge of information on the Net and this can be an intimidating and frightening experience. For many students it is difficult to find the right information – hours can be spent fruitlessly surfing, often achieving little for the time and effort spent.

For many also, it can be difficult to effectively use the information for their task. With the impact of information technology, comes the need to develop in students the ability to be discerning and to critically evaluate the value of information to the task in hand. Information overload can easily overwhelm and confuse the learner with irrelevant and useless material that may then distract from the actual task in hand.

> **What strategies can we teach our students so they will feel confident in dealing with large amountsof information?**

How to achieve "Critical Thinkers"

Develop problem-solving techniques:
In our daily lives – at home, at work or at play, we are constantly making choices – making choices based on new information combined with prior knowledge. Making choices enhances the ability to solve more complex problems. By providing our students with opportunities to solve problems, we are teaching them how to solve problems they will face throughout their lives – at TAFE and College, University, in the workplace, in recreation and in the home - the skills for lifelong learning.

Develop effective research strategies:
Researchers are suggesting that the Information Process is an effective approach to problem solving and as a useful strategy to guide the research process.

> *Knowledge and understanding of the process they are using will assist students to comprehend their own learning and enable them to apply that same process to any problem solving situation, i.e., a tool for lifelong learning.*

The ability to critically define the task - to brainstorm prior to learning, to devise headings and subheadings appropriate to the topic, has always been a critical aspect of the research process. These skills remain equally relevant regardless of whether the source is print or non-print material.

Locating resources has taken on a new dimension with the advent of electronic sources of information.

As teachers, we must be aware of focusing on specific skills required to locate, select and reject resources from non-print sources. Students must be able to skim and scan from books as well as screen.

Selecting information from the located resources requires students to critically analyse the information for its relevance and appropriateness to the task. Often, an interesting article that does not really address the topic may overwhelm students. How well students have **analysed** and clarified their task is reflected in the information selected. Frequently students do not answer the question because they have not thoroughly understood their task and have been sidetracked by interesting, but irrelevant information.

The ability to **organise** the located information in note form under appropriate headings and subheadings is relevant to both print and non-print sources. But how is this note taking done? Are the notes hand written? From book or screen? Are the notes "cut and pasted" on the screen to a template? Are these digital notes organised into headings and subheadings?

> *By building progressive checkpoints into assignment criteria, teachers can, to a large extent, monitor the originality of the work.*

Synthesising the new information with prior knowledge is when students "make the links" and begin to develop original ideas and solutions to the set task.

Creating the solution, or developing original ideas, then presenting the outcome to an appropriate audience is of significant importance to the student. A task that is interesting, challenging and authentic will result in the student feeling a great sense of satisfaction and achievement in the presentation of his/her efforts.

> *Evaluating the effectiveness of the student's own participation in the process, and evaluating the effectiveness of the student's completion of the task, is a vital part of the research process.*

It is from this evaluation the student can learn what he/she did well, and what skills must be learnt to make the process more effective next time.

Assignment setting: It is of the utmost importance that students are given the opportunity to solve problems, or to offer original ideas when completing an assignment or project. A task that is problem-based, has relevance to real life, and is of interest to the students, will considerably motivate and enthuse students.

> *A problem provides the opportunity for students to create original thoughts and ideas, rather than to just "read and regurgitate" the ideas of others.*

A problem-based task also enhances the opportunity for students to engage in higher order thinking skills.

Minimising plagiarism: Again, a problem to solve reduces the opportunity, and need, for plagiarism. Once the student has researched what others think about the topic, they must then offer their own solution, based on the new information and their existing knowledge.

Bookmarked Internet sites: Considerable time can be saved and frustration avoided for students, if sites can be pre-selected and then "bookmarked" or added to "Favourites" by either teacher or teacher-librarian. Organising these addresses into folders can simplify locating relevant sites quickly and easily. Bookmarked sites can provide a starting point, enabling students to locate appropriate information without aimless searching.

> *Teaching students to evaluate the potential value of a site from the "blurb" or annotation following the address, assists students to develop the ability to critically assess a site without following the link, and so saving time.*

WebQuests: are intriguing open-ended problems that provide a valuable web-based learning curriculum approach. Students work collaboratively whilst engaging in higher order thinking skills, and use the web to develop solutions to the problem.

As pre-developed teacher-friendly strategies that are problem-based, WebQuests are highly motivating and challenging to students. Once having tried existing WebQuests, there is always the possibility of developing original challenges.

Ask an Expert: The use of email to dialogue with "experts", authors, heroes, students in schools from around the globe, provides a stimulating and challenging avenue for students to explore a topic or issue, to pose questions or to challenge an opinion.

The implementation of a planned Information Literacy program throughout the school will enhance the development of attributes of a lifelong learner, enabling the student to cope confidently and efficiently in a complex and uncertain future.

3] Giant Leaps and Small Steps

Megan Perry and Debbie Leatheam

"Smart questions are essential technology for those who venture onto the Information Highway. Without strong questioning skills, you are just a passenger on someone else's tour bus. You may be on the highway, but someone else is doing the driving." (McKenzie 2000, 7)

Teachers today are overwhelmed with multiple competing interests and divergent challenges that include restructuring, funding shortfalls, transformative pedagogical movements, benchmarking, exceptional parental expectations, place on the yearly academic league table, legal liability, performance-based appraisal, lack of promotional opportunity, and of course the challenge of learning to use, and then integrate, new information and communication technologies into an already overburdened curriculum.

However, exacerbated by massive curriculum restructuring, technological, and pedagogical change forced from above, teachers are now faced with the reality of change being the only constant in their very busy lives.

Whilst the integration of information and communications technologies can be seen to be the catalyst that is facilitating the transformation of schools, the reality is that teachers are struggling with both the skills required to master the new technologies, and more importantly, they struggle with the skills required to apply technology in a way that meets the needs of the learner, who does not remember a time when computers did not exist.

The promise of computer technology in schools has in many cases been disappointing, as teachers and administrators have not understood that technology alone does not create change. In addition, as Alan J Kay reminded us in 1994, "… any problems that schools cannot solve without machines, they cannot solve with them." (Pearlman 1994, 43) Whilst Serim, (2001, 6) argues that "The integration of information and communications technology can however, facilitate a new way of thinking and learning".

In an era when most students have access to Internet and Intranet resources, the traditional content-based assignment, which asks students to identify, list, describe, summarise and recall facts or content, becomes redundant.

> **Too often we hear the disappointment in teachers' voices when they describe assignments that are merely 'cut and pasted' and chunked and diced from the Internet.**

Teachers are becoming all too aware of sites such as: www.freeessays.com, www.planetessays.com, www.A+essays.com ,www.schoolsux.com, www.megaessays.com, and the resultant complexity of issues in marking plagiarized responses.

Now, more so than ever, teachers feel the enormous pressure of increasing student performance at yearly external exams, and are frustrated by the lack of qualitative and quantitative research that explicitly outlines *how* the integration of information and communication technologies and information skills can actually achieve higher student results.

Yet, some teachers are bravely recognizing the need to master that, which is shaping both our clientele and the world in which we all live.

Specifically this paper outlines how, in developing a curriculum specific Intranet, teachers were encouraged to look at changing the questions they were asking their students, and to embed and scaffold computing and information skills within the assignment process.

Within the context of The King's School Library in a secondary school environment, the following process was devised to facilitate the development of worthy and developmentally appropriate student assignments.

It has long been recognized that teaching skills outside a curriculum context is of little value and necessarily, libraries that exist on the periphery of the curriculum are less relevant than those that hold the curriculum as "core business".

The process is based around collaboration between the Head of Department or the classroom teacher and the Teacher Librarian.

A vital element of this collaboration is the power of conversation and mutual recognition and respect for the knowledge and understandings that each brings to the process.

In the absence of compelling models for secondary schools, a curriculum focused, student centred Intranet evolved, which provided students with an easily navigable interface where all assignments are published. Scaffolded within each assignment is information and computing skills, web based, print and other media resources, templates, ideas and teacher guidance.

The following web based resources provide a common foundation and a common scaffold from which to work with teachers and Heads of Department:

- Information Literacy Process

- The King's School 7-12 Department Programmes

- The King's School Computing Skills continua

- The King's School Information Services Assignment Guide

- The King's School Information Services Bibliography Guide

- The King's School Computer Use Policy

- The Kings School Plagiarism Policy

- Bloom's Taxonomy guide

- Board of Studies Key word glossary

- Gardner's Multiple Intelligences

- The King's School Information Services Text Types

This consistent approach across all departments and throughout the school year reinforces the integration of the information and computing skills across the whole school. It is when these skills are integrated within authentic assessment tasks that their real value is recognized.

Broadly defined the collaborative process between the teacher and Teacher Librarian includes the following elements:

Process:
1. **Collaboration** – ongoing discussion
   a.   Defining expected outcomes;
   b.   Content area and focus question.

2. Resourcing
   a. Information seeking strategies;
   b. Locating and accessing suitable information sources;
   c. Print and vertical file, Newspapers/Periodicals, Online databases, Video and Web resources.

3. Question design
   a. Selecting and analysing tools;
   b. Use of information;
   c. Blooms Taxonomy of Learning;
   d. Gardner Multiple Intelligences;
   e. Computing skills;
   f. Information skills;
   g. Other scaffolds.

4. Organisation and Synthesis
   a. Text type;
   b. Presentation expectations;
   c. Marking scheme, check outcomes;
   d. Publish to Intranet Assignments in Progress.

5. Review with teacher
   a. Book lessons allowing for assignment introduction, information and computing and information skills acquisition;
   b. Publish to Intranet Current Assignments;
   c. Evaluation.

Collaboration

The value of conversation is intrinsically important at the initial questioning stage. Teachers and Teacher Librarians bring to the process very different but vital skills. Obviously the teacher has a direct interest in the syllabus requirements.

Teacher Librarians have a school wide focus on information and computing skills and can see the broader picture of where and when it is appropriate to introduce or reinforce a skill previously taught. Ideally, an information and computing skills curriculum map locates where and when skills are introduced, reinforced and mainstreamed. This document provides an effective guide for the teacher and Teacher Librarian as they explore the assignment task.

Resourcing

The Teacher Librarian identifies the most appropriate available resources. It is important to ensure that students are exposed to all media, not just the web, and to also recognize that each media type requires the acquisition of specific skills.

Question Design

To design an effective question teachers need access to thinking tools such as Bloom's Taxonomy of Learning and Gardner's Multiple Intelligences. In addition, the Teacher Librarian identifies within the information and computing skills continua, the skills that should be introduced, reinforced or mainstreamed.

Other scaffolding strategies can also be discussed at this stage. These may include visual tools, templates for writing particular text types, sample answers, etc.

The following template provides the teacher with a quick thinking guideline as they explore the task. This document is easily accessible from the Intranet. In many cases "less is more", and teachers need a 'quick hit' to clarify and pull the package together.

	Checklist	**Tools**
Aim	What exactly do you want the boys to research and learn and why?	**Learning activities** Do the boys understand how the research segment underpins and complements the other activities in the unit of work?
Outcomes	What do you want the students to know at the end of the task? What are the relevant outcomes from the syllabus? Are they clearly identified?	Board of Studies Outcomes
The Task	Have you asked a clear question? Does the question explain what you expect the boys to produce /achieve? Is the question pitched at appropriate levels? Blooms Taxonomy of learning identifies levels of questions that require the boys to move from *knowledge* (level 1) to *evaluation* (level 6). Which information skills need to be built into the assignment?	What existing knowledge do the boys have? Do the boys need an extra lesson to acquire the skills necessary to complete the task? i.e., PowerPoint, scanning, Office Suite, etc? Information Literacy Overview
Presentation	Have you clearly identified which text type you require? Have you identified when the task is due. Day? In person? Date? Where? Time? Word length? Include a Bibliography reminder and link key words to the Key Word Glossary where relevant.	Multiple Intelligences Text Types

	Checklist	Tools
Marking Criteria	Have you linked your marking criteria to the outcomes you have identified? Does the marking scheme properly reflect the requirements of the question?	
Policies	Include School policies on Plagiarism and Assessment.	The King's School Plagiarism and Assessment policies
Resources	Have you identified specific books, periodicals, web links that may assist the boys?	Web Link (specifically chosen for schools) Library Catalogue for print and audiovisual resources.

Organisation and Synthesis

To ensure student success in manipulating the language effectively, and engaging the audience appropriately, it is vital that they develop competency in using a variety of text types and presentation styles. To expect a student to produce a written essay, web pages or a drama script without explicitly teaching the skills required is setting the student up for failure. It is now imperative that all teachers teach all literacies.

Review with Teacher

The connection between teacher expectations and outcomes are discussed and clearly identified. Linking the marking criteria effectively to the outcomes allows the teacher to identify the priorities of the assignment. For example, the focus of an assignment may in fact be in the skill of developing a bibliography, or accessing relevant periodical articles. Necessarily, this area will be more heavily weighted in the marking criteria.

Mapping the process and identifying the number and frequency of lessons to cover the task and associated skills instruction should be planned at this stage, as should the presentation requirements. Included within each assignment are the school policies regarding assessment, plagiarism and the preferred bibliography style This consistent approach encourages boys to transfer skills across curriculum areas and to recognize the whole school approach to assessment.

In publishing the finished product with all associated links to the school Intranet, all students, staff and parents have access to the fully scaffolded assignment.

The evaluation process is vital, as both the teacher and Teacher Librarian see the relative strengths and weaknesses of both the task and the students' skills. It is only when the Teacher Librarian is involved in the evaluation process that the power of the collaboration can be appreciated.

Example Assignments

- Year 7: Famous Scientists
- Year 10: Genetics
- Year 8: Advertising

(Editor's note: the example assignments mentioned above may be found in Chapter 10 – *Problem-based Tasks.*)

The success of The King's School approach is based on an acceptance of the need to scaffold and embed both information and computing skills within each assignment. Additionally, school based policies underpin the 'whole school approach' and lend weight and integrity to the process which is based on a constantly evolving and collaborative model.

References

McKenzie, J. (2000)   *Beyond Technology. Questioning, Research and the Information Literate School.* FNO Press: Bellingham Washington.

Serim, F. (2001)   Our task: Seizing the Opportunity *MultiMedia Schools* 8 no 2 March/April 2001 p. 6.

Developing a Learning Culture

Peter Ellyard

'Life-long learning' and 'organisational learning' became buzzwords in the 1990s. It is recognised that both individuals and organisations must learn continuously in order to adapt to changing circumstances and to develop new skills and capabilities to thrive in a rapidly changing world. There is also recognition that any enterprise that seeks to be successful in the knowledge-based industrial system of the twenty-first century needs to be led and managed in ways that maximise organisational learning. This is increasingly so, because as contract work grows, rapid staff turnover can significantly undermine organisational memory.

However, life-long learning and organisational learning are only two facets of the learning culture, which must be developed. As part of my work with Victorian principals I developed a pedagogy for a learning culture in collaboration with the learning consultant, Dr Julia Atkin.

> *If learning is to be maximised a new model and pedagogy of learning – a new learning culture – is needed.*

This learning culture should contain eight elements:

- Life-long learning
- Learner-driven learning
- Just-in-time learning
- Customised learning
- Transformative learning
- Collaborative learning
- Contextual learning
- Learning to learn

Life-long Learning (LLL)

The world's education systems are slowly modifying what can be termed an 'early-in-life' or 'front-end' system of education into a life-long one.

> *In the past, education in developed countries has been dedicated to teaching and learning during the first third of life, and in much of the rest of the world it has been for a ten-year period from the approximate age of five to fifteen years.*

With the exceptions of some continuing adult education for relatively few people, formal learning over the remaining two-thirds of life has been ignored. At Present, countries such as Australia have a hybrid of the 'early-in-life' and 'life-long' systems, and the transformation has been largely problem-centred and ad hoc. There is no vision of the nature of a preferred life-long system of education that describes the essential ingredients of LLL systems, and where and how such systems differ from early-in-life systems.

> *Most formal learning has traditionally occurred in this early-in-life period of compulsory education.*

Under these circumstances learning could be force-fed into (often unwilling) educational customers. At the end of the twentieth century schools, together with hospitals and prisons, were remnant factories whose designs and operations were still influenced by the time and motion studies of Frederick Winslow Taylor and the mass production of Henry Ford. Manufacturing has moved forward from 'economies of scale' to 'economies of scope'. Not so the schools.

Compulsory education developed at a time when most jobs were low skilled and work places wanted docile, unquestioning takers of orders. It did not matter if students were so alienated by school that they vowed they would never expose themselves to the education system again.

> **Now we are developing a rapidly changing, knowledge-based society, and this early-in-life learning is being replaced by life-long learning.**

Adult learners will not put up with the autocratic 'teacher-knows-best' form of education experienced by most of us in childhood and which, unfortunately, still persists in too many educational situations. A pedagogy is now needed to ensure that learning is enjoyable, or that the context of learning encourages students to persist with less enjoyable learning pathways.

> **Life-long learning facilitates flexible career paths, promotes adaptability and empowers the personal development required in a rapidly changing world.**

The adoption of a full culture of life-long learning will have profound implications for what goes on in the primary and secondary education systems, which will need to change as much as work places have. If primary and secondary education systems are no longer required to provide the basic quantum of knowledge and expertise needed for the whole of life they will be relieved of a major burden that is stifling them. There will be no need for overcrowded curricula since people have the whole of life to learn and are not restricted to just a few learning years early in life. With a system of life-long learning no longer would it be necessary to pack into the years of formal schooling most of the knowledge that is needed for success in life.

> **What is important in an LLL system is that people leave formal education with their early childhood desire to be a life-long learner still intact.**

There should be a love of learning, and people should be capable of life-long learning because they have the skills such as literacy and numeracy to access knowledge. People should also have the confidence to be life-long learners.

If there is already a love of learning, a desire to learn and a capability and confidence to learn, then people will take the opportunities to learn when they are offered.

Much of our most important learning occurs before we go to school. Perhaps one could say that an important example of the denial of human rights is that children do not have the right to pick their own parents!

> *Children who have parents who are poor teachers can be disadvantaged for life.*

Some formal education systems in other countries, such as a famous program in Missouri in the United States, are recognising this fact and are providing resources to assist parents to become more effective educators. Two-year-old children are natural learners; they cannot stop learning, their desire seems insatiable. For two-year-olds, learning is not only essential it is also fun.

> *However, by the time many children are halfway through secondary school all the pleasure of learning has vanished and with it much of the desire.*

Motivation has become driven by external factors such as exams rather than by curiosity. That is, the natural endowment of life-long learning has been converted into compulsory, early-in-life learning, which has killed much of the pleasure but, more importantly, kills the motivation to be a life-long learner.

> *We should ensure that children arrive at school as enthusiastic, life-long learners driven by curiosity, and that they stay that way throughout their lives.*

When many children first arrive at school they are already showing symptoms of advantage or disadvantage that some never overcome, despite the efforts of the education system.

In addition, schools spend large amounts of money on remedial education, much of which would be unnecessary if schools went into the home in their communities and helped parents to become good teachers of their own children. A preventative program would produce net savings to the education system as well as providing a huge bonus for social and economic equity.

More effort and resources need to be spent on the early childhood stage to give all children an equal opportunity to become life-long learners and to overcome any disadvantages which may result from the different capacities parents have to be effective and inspiring teachers of their own children. Most parents want to give their children the best but the capacities to do so differ markedly. Teachers could visit families in their homes and help develop effective teaching skills in the parents. It is certain that the cost savings, both in remedial education and the gains to national income and equity, would be considerable.

> **People who currently 'fail' in the education system are the ones who currently suffer most in an era of rapid change.**

With a system of LLL they would have second and third chances to develop their career and personal development paths (their future learning) by conscious choice and by negotiation with education providers.

Learner-Driven Learning (LDL)

In traditional schooling learning is initiated by teachers. The average two-year-old's learning is driven by curiosity – by the need to know.

> **Wherever possible, all learning should be made learner-initiated and learner-managed.**

Learner-driven learning (LDL) encourages independent learning that replaces the dependence of teacher-driven learning. Independent learners will then be able to become interdependent learners. Modern technology that allows the learner to use the Internet, the CD-ROM and a host of other educational tools now permits the learner to initiate and manage learning.

> **The development of a system of LDL will transform the nature of teaching.**

Technology is making the old demarcation between teachers and librarians more and more blurred. In the next ten years or so it is likely that there will be an integration of the traditional roles of teacher and librarian into a single profession to assist learner-driven, life-long learners. The new professional, called a 'knowledge navigator', could assist learners to seek and find knowledge by gaining access to a wide variety of knowledge resources, and to enrich and affirm that knowledge and learning where appropriate. There is also another future role for the former teacher professional: as a mentor who is responsible for assisting and inspiring personal development.

LDL will also be assisted by the development of greater student autonomy. It is likely that a system – such as the 'Educard", similar to a universal health insurance card – will give students the right to access learning from a wide variety of educational providers. The power of educational providers to control the education system is drawing to an end.

> **From now on the customers, or the parents of very young customers, will have a greater say in shaping the education system.**

It is important that they do so because each learner must assume responsibility for their life-long learning. This means that they should choose what they learn, when they learn and how they learn. It is time for the education system to recognise this fact and plan positively for an LDL educational system.

Just-In-Time Learning (JITL)

The average two-year-old wants to learn immediately when seeking an answer to a question. This is curiosity-driven learning and it is the best way to learn. The concept of just-in-time (JIT) commenced in the manufacturing and retail sectors as an alternative method of production and operation, which meant that enterprises did not need large stockpiles of all the components required for assembling a particular product. Components were sourced at a rate that was 'just in time' for the production. This is manufacturing interdependence.

> ***This concept should now be applied to education to ensure that learning mostly occurs when there is a high motivation to learn.***

Modern technology permits us to provide such a learning system. Educators and business now have both the responsibility and opportunity to create it. Just-in-time learning (JITL) has the capacity to reinforce both LLL and LDL. The net result of these changes will be that curiosity will again become a driving force for learning.

Customised Learning (CusL)

Just as people have preferences for using their left or right hands, so they learn and think in different ways depending on the part of the brain they prefer to use in their learning processes.

> ***People are different and so think and learn in different ways.***

Some are visphiles, some are audiophiles, some prefer to learn by right-brain processes and some prefer left-brain processes. There are quadrants in the brain and each is associated with particular learning processes.

Dr Julia Atkin, the Australian education and learning specialist, has described the difference between the quadrants as: 'upper left' – learning by gaining information and facts; 'lower left' – learning by being able to do, acting out, applying; 'lower right' – learning by feeling emotions, experiencing and doing; 'upper right' – learning by making connections, understand and insight. While all of us use more than one quadrant and many of us use three or all four, we all prefer to use some quadrants more than others and we learn fastest by using our favoured ways of learning.

> **These individual differences are not reflected in the way teaching and learning is conducted in schools.**

Our education system also does little to encourage us to develop whole-brain learning capabilities.

Because of the encapsulation of knowledge in the written word in the past, education and learning have favoured people with preferred left-brain thinking and learning processes. Mark Twain once said: 'My education was only interrupted by my schooling'. It is likely that he was a right-brained learner and the book-driven learning processes of the late nineteenth century favoured people who were left-brain learners. It is possible that there is an association between the increased dominance by left-brain processes in education, and particularly in learning from books, and the disappearance of the desire to learn in many young people, and with it the desire to be a life-long learner.

If right-brained thinkers are not successful in being appointed to senior positions in organisations, and this often occurs because people are chosen in the main according to their management skills, then the organisation will become over-managed and under-led.

> **Vision is a product of right-brain processes.**

Organisations which do not encourage right-brained thinking will lack vision, therefore customising learning for all thinking preferences will mean a better balance rather than the over-dominance of left-brained thinkers and processors which is found in organisations today. To get more organisational vision we need affirmative action for right-brained thinking.

> *With the disappearance of the desire to learn we lose a basic capacity to adapt in a modern, rapidly changing world.*

Failure to become literate or numerate ensures failure in a modern technological world. But this is likely to be at least a partial reflection of the fact that the current education system has tended to favour left-brain processors.

We all know stories of brilliant people who drop out of school because they could not or would not learn. In many cases the learning opportunities were totally unsuitable to their personal learning styles.

> *Modern technology now enables the packaging of learning modules to suit people with different preferred styles, and learners can choose the way they wish to learn.*

Technology can provide learning pathways to suit individual learners who can select educational learning options most suited to their own personal learning pathways. Imagine an educational supermarket with many customised learning packages sitting on the shelves. Learner-driven learners choose the package appropriate for their preferred learning and thinking styles, and therefore are able to maximise their own learning.

> *Thus modern technology can permit different learning and thinking preferences to be catered for, and for whole-brain thinking and learning to be promoted.*

Transformative Learning (TL)

> *Learning should transform people and challenge and change belief systems and behavioural patterns to meet new needs and opportunities and to overcome disabilities and disadvantages.*

It is important that assessment systems be instituted which measure transformation as well as evaluate knowledge. The transformative component of learning is therefore critical in the world of rapid change. Often politicians use the word 're-training' as the solution to the problem of a lack of adaptability to change. Apart from the fact that the word 'training' is a totally inappropriate word, training is not what is needed: what is needed is learning, and continuous life-long, learner-driven, just-in-time and transformative learning. Training is a nineteenth-century concept that has passed its 'use-by' date. Nowadays this concept of training might be suitable for dogs but it is not suitable for people who need to think for themselves in their work, and to continuously grow and transform themselves.

Contextual Learning (ContL)

> *Our experience tells us that learning is most effective if it occurs in an environment, which makes the learning relevant to the experience and expectations of the learner.*

Learning rarely occurred this way in schools of the twentieth century. Traditionally, learning was centred on promoting knowledge in ways that were often removed from using that knowledge in life. We used to sit in classrooms and be told about the nature of things.

> *The best way of learning in context is to create an experiential situation that validates and affirms the learning.*

Modern technology has the capacity to create an awesome variety of virtual reality processes that can improve learning and emphasise learning by doing, learning by experimenting and learning by trying and failing. Learning can also go to appropriate places; for example, learning about animal liberation/vegetarianism could take place in an abattoir.

Learning To Learn (LTL)

Until recently, if one assessed the time devoted to these educational activities the result seemed to assume that people did not need to learn how to learn and think.

> *If people know more about how they learn they will be better placed to improve their thinking and learning capacities.*

All learners need to have the capability to understand how they think and learn and to develop their capacity in both these fields. This will assist them to plan more effectively and drive their own learning. It develops the capability in individuals and groups to understand plan more effectively, to manage and realise their own learning.

References

Alexander, C., Ishikawa, S., Silverstein, M.J. et al., (1977). *A Pattern Language,* Oxford University Press, New York.

Alexander, C., Silverstein, M., Angel, S., Ishikawa, S and Abrams, D., (1975).*The Oregon Experiment,* Oxford University Press, New York.

Atwood, M., (1985). *The Handmaid's Tale,* Vintage Books, London.

Australian Bureau of Statistics, (1987). Artwork: *A Report on Australians Working in the Arts,* Australia Council, Canberra.

Ball, C., (1989). *Towards an Enterprising Culture: A Challenge for Education and Training,* Educational Monograph No. 4, Centre for Educational Research and Innovation, Organisation for Economic Cooperation and Development, Paris.

Bell, D., (1973). *The Coming of Post-Industrial society: A Venture in Social Forecasting,* Basic Books, New York.

Bly, R., (1991). *Iron John: A Book about Men,* Element, London.

Boulding, K.E., (1966), The economics of the coming Spaceship Earth. In H. Jarret (ed.), *Environmental Quality in a Growing Economy,* John Hopkins University Press, Baltimore, Maryland, 3-14.

Boyden, S., (1987). *Western Civilization in Biological Perspective: Patterns in Biohistory,* Oxford University Press, Oxford.

Boyden, S and Shirlow, M., (1989). Ecological sustainability and the quality of life. In V. Brown (ed.), *A Sustainable Healthy Future, Towards an Ecology of Health,* La Trobe University and the Commission for the Future, Melbourne.

Buckminster-Fuller, R., (1969). *Operating Manual for Spaceship Earth,* University of Southern Illinois Press, Carbondale, Ill.

Campbell, J. (1993). *Myths to Live By,* Penguin, Arkana.

Carmichael, L., (1994). (the Carmichael Report), *Raising the Standard: Beyond Entry Level Skills,* Australian Government Publishing Service, Canberra.

Covey, S. R., (1992). *Principle-centred Leadership,* Simon & Schuster, London.

Department of Trade, Mission Members to the ACTU and the TDC, (1987). *Australia Reconstructed,* Australian Government Publishing Service, Canberra.

Finn, B., (1991). (the Finn Report), *Young People's Participation in Post Compulsory Education and Training,* Australian Government Publishing Service, Canberra.

Ford, G. W. (Bill), (1996). Personal communication.

Gibson, W., (1984). *Neuromancer,* Ace Books, New York.

Goethe, Johan Wolfgang von. (1967). *Faust: A Tragedy,* translated in the original meters by Bayard Taylor, Random House, New York.

Hamel, G. and Prahalad, C.K., (1994). *Competing for the Future,* Harvard Business School Press, Mass.

Hampden-Turner, C. and Trompenaars, F., (1994). *The Seven Cultures of Capitalism,* Piatkus, London.

Hampden-Turner, C. and Trompenaars, F., (1997). *Mastering the Infinite Game,* Capstone Publishing, Oxford.

Henderson, Hazel, (1992). *Paradigms in Progress: Life Beyond Economics,* Knowledge Systems, Illinois.

Illich, I., (1978). *Disabling Professions,* Marian Boyars, London.

Illich, I., (1976). *Limits to Medicine,* Penguin, Harmondsworth.

Kirby, P. E. F., (1985). (the Kirby Report), *Report of the Committee of Enquiry into Labour Market Programs,* Australian Government Publishing Service, Canberra.

Koestler, A., (1978). *Janus: A Summing Up,* Hutchinson, London.

Lam, M. (ed.), (1991). *Use Your Initiative: Enterprise Skills for the Future,* Commission for the Future, Australian Government Publishing Service, Canberra.

Lindell, M., (1989). Convivial communities: an optimist's view. In V. Brown (ed.), *A Sustainable Healthy Future, Towards an Ecology of Health,* La Trobe University and the Commission for the Future, Melbourne.

Lovelock, J., (1995). *Gaia: A New Look at Life on Earth,* Oxford University Press, Oxford.

McDonough, W., (n.d.) *The Hanover Principles: Design for Sustainability,* 3rd edn, McDonough and Partners, Charlottesville, Virginia, USA.

Mayer, E. (1992). (the Mayer Report), *Key Competencies,* Australian Government Publishing Service, Canberra.

Modjeska, D., (1990). *Poppy,* Penguin, Ringwood, Vic.

Mortimer, D and Lawriwsky, M., (1997). *Going for Growth: Business Programs for Investment, Innovation and Exports,* Review of Business Programs, Department of Industry, Science and Tourism, Canberra.

Murray, W. H., (1951). *The Scottish Himalayan Expedition,* J. H. Dent & Sons Ltd, London.

National Academy of Sciences, (1975). *Underexploited Tropical Plants with Promising Economic Value,* report of an *ad hoc* panel of the Advisory committee on Technology Innovation, F. R. Ruskin, Washington, DC.

National computer Board (Singapore), (1992). A *Vision of an Intelligent Island: The IT2000 Report,* SNP Publishers, Singapore.

Peres, Shimon, (2000). *A Taste of Eden.* Australian, January 3, 2000.

Popcorn, F. (1992). *The Popcorn Report,* Random House, Milsons Point, NSW,

Richardson, D., (1988). *Esperanto, Learning and Using the International Language,* Orcas, Eastsound, Washington.

Singer, P., (1981). *The Expanding Circle: Ethics and Sociobiology,* Farrer, Straus & Giroux, New York.

Smart, B., (1992). *Modern Conditions, Post Modern Controversies,* Routledge, London.

Stewart, J. (ed.), (1991). 'Technological change and industrial policy: are we in the race?', *Federalism and Public Policy: The management of Science and Technology,* Australian Science and Technology council, Occasional Paper No. 18, September 1991, 5-15.

Tacey, D., (1992). *ReEnchantment: The New Australian Spirituality,* HarperCollins, Sydney, with 2000 Centre, Canberra.

Thompson, W. I. (ed.), (1987). *Gaia: A Way of Knowing. Political Implications of the New Biology,* Lindisfarne Press, Mass.

Toffler, A., (1971). *Future Shock,* Pan Books, London.

U Thant, (1970). 'The human environment and world order', speech delivered at the University of Texas, 17 May, 1970, *UN Monthly Chronicle,* June, VII (6).

United Nations Development Program, (1996). *Human Development Report,* Oxford University Press, New York.

Ventura, M., (1989). The Age of Endarkment, In *Whole Earth Review,* Winter.

Ward, Barbara, (1976). *The Home of Man,* Andre Deutsch. London.

World Commission on Environment and Development (the Brundland commission), (1987). *Our Common Future,* Oxford University Press, Oxford.

The Affective Dimension of Information Literacy

Dianne Oberg

Introduction

The information literacy process is a kind of inquiry-based or problem-based learning that plays a critical role in developing information literate learners.

> *In order for students to have rewarding experiences through the information literacy process, teachers and librarians need to provide instructional guidance that is affective as well as cognitive in focus.*

Teachers and librarians need to have a deep understanding of how learners experience the information literacy process and about how learning through investigation can be facilitated.

In the past two decades, process-based models of information literacy instruction have been developed in many parts of the world including the United Kingdom, the United States, Australia, and Canada.

> *However, the effective implementation of such models depends on teachers and librarians understanding that students vary in the level of abstraction that they can handle, that students are active learners building or constructing their knowledge as they use information and that students are experiencing changes in feelings as well as changes of thoughts as they use information.*

This issue is explored through an analysis of the Australian process model presented by Jenny Ryan and Steph Capra (2001b, 2001b), using research related to the implementation of this and similar models in primary, middle, and secondary schools.

Process-based models of information literacy instruction support a view of information literacy as an opportunity for students to experience learning through inquiry and problem-solving characterized by exploration and risk–taking, by curiosity and motivation, by engagement in critical and creative thinking, and by connections with real life situations and real audiences (AASL, 1999; Bush, 1998; Harada, 1998; Schroeder & Zarinnia, 2001).

What is regarded as exemplary library instruction has changed over the past thirty years: during the 1960s and 1970s, a source approach; through the 1980s, a pathfinder approach; and today, a process approach.

> *The process approach to teaching the information literacy process emphasizes thinking about information and using information within a problem-solving perspective.*

It does not discard the knowledge from earlier approaches, such as the knowledge of tools, sources, and search strategies, but it does emphasize that this knowledge is to be developed within the teaching of thinking and problem solving.

The process approach to develop information literacy goes beyond the location of information to the use of information, beyond the answering of a specific question to the seeking of evidence to shape a topic.

> *It considers the process of a search for information as well as the product of the search.*

It calls for an awareness of the complexity of learning from information: learning from information is not a routine or standardized task, and it involves the affective as well as the cognitive domains.

The process model is theory-based and grounded in research from the fields of education and of library and information studies (LIS). From education, comes learning theory and from LIS, information seeking behaviour theory.

For example, from education comes the knowledge that learners vary in the level of abstraction that they can handle, depending on their cognitive development and their prior knowledge and experience. From education also comes the constructivist concept of learners actively building or constructing their knowledge and of learners experiencing changes in feelings as well as changes of thoughts as they use information.

From LIS comes the knowledge that users of information progress through levels of question specificity, from vague notions of information need to clearly defined needs or questions, and that ...

... users are more successful in the search process if they have a realistic understanding of the information system and of the information problem.

An Australian Model
for Teaching the Information literacy process:

There are many process-based information literacy models. In Britain, we see the work of Ann Irving, Michael Marland and James Herring; in the United States, we see the work of Carol Kuhlthau, of Barbara Stripling and Judy Pitts, and of Marjorie Pappas and Ann Tepe.

This work is reflected in the model for teaching the information literacy process developed in my province in Canada, *Focus on Research* (Alberta Education, 1990). It is also reflected in the Australian information literacy model called the Information Process (Ryan & Capra, 2001a)

This Information Process is a six-stage model (see Figure 1). Below, I suggest some strategies for guiding learners through the information literacy process, for each of the six stages in the Information Process model. In this section of the paper, I have used the term 'teachers' to refer to both classroom teachers and teacher-librarians, working in collaboration with the students in the classroom and the library.

An earlier version of this paper, based on an analysis of a Canadian model, *Focus on Research*, was presented at the IFLA Conference in Bangkok, Thailand (Oberg, 1999).

THE INFORMATION PROCESS

DEFINING   In this phase the student formulates questions, analyses and clarifies the requirements of the problem or task. This is the first in the Information Literacy cycle. As a result of new learnings and understandings, this phase is frequently revisited during the entire process to refine and re-define the problem or task for further clarification.

LOCATING   The student identifies potential sources of information, and is able to locate and access a variety of resources from multiple formats.

SELECTING/ ANALYSING   The student analyses, selects and rejects information appropriate to the problem or task from the located resources.

ORGANISING/ SYNTHESISING   The student critically analyses and organises the gathered information, synthesises new learnings incorporating prior knowledge to develop original insights to a problem or task.

CREATING/ PRESENTING   The student creates a response to the problem or task, presenting the solution to an appropriate audience.

EVALUATING   In this final phase, the student critically evaluates the effectiveness of his/her ability to complete the assigned task, and identifies future learning needs.

Throughout the Process ...

The Information Literacy Process is a cyclic process, with some steps being revisited from time to time as a result of new insights.

> *Reviewing the Information Literacy Process is a critical element for helping students to understand research as a learning process and to develop their metacognitive abilities, for both 'thinking about thinking' and for 'thinking about feeling.'*

Work on metacognition began with Vygotsky in the 1920s. Metacognition encompasses all the thinking that we do to evaluate our own mental processes and to plan for appropriate use of these processes to meet the demands of the situation. Metacognitive knowledge includes knowledge of person, task, and strategy, that is, knowledge of one's capacity to learn, about the nature of what is to be learned, and about actions that one can take to aid one's thinking (Flavell, 1979).

Work on helping students to develop their abilities to think about, evaluate and monitor their feelings began much later, in the 1970s. Thinking about feeling, termed "emotional literacy" (Toben, 1999) or "emotional intelligence" can be defined as:

> *The ability to perceive, access, and generate emotions so as to assist thought, to understand emotions and emotional knowledge, and to reflectively regulate emotions so as to promote emotional and intellectual growth.* (Slavoney & Sluyter, 1997)

Young students, in their first few years in school, for example, are less likely to have developed these metacognitive and emotional abilities but they can be helped to do so, within the limits of their intellectual and emotional maturation.

Older students as well, need to be assisted to understand their feelings as well as their thinking as they work through the information literacy process.

McGregor (1994) found that even bright high school seniors in their 11th year in school needed assistance in learning to think about their thinking, while Loerke (1992) pointed out that graduate students may be unaware that feelings of confusion and frustration are a natural part of the information literacy process.

When teachers pose questions about thinking and feeling and allow students to reflect upon their learning progress, students' personal growth is enhanced. Students' motivation to learn is also enhanced when such activities honour diverse learning styles and perspectives.

> *Teachers should use a model of the information literacy process on a consistent basis and explicitly call the students' attention to the model and to the particular stage at which they are working.*

Other useful strategies for reviewing the information literacy process include class discussions, journal writing, and making timelines as well as ongoing and retrospective analyses of the data generated through such activities.

Stage 1: Defining

In the Defining stage, students are given the opportunity to get an image of the whole information literacy process; getting a sense of the project as a whole supports student success.

> *Engaging students in the Defining stage is crucial.*

Even with the youngest researchers, teachers can have them identify what they know and what they want to know about the topic, generate ideas about potential information sources, and discuss potential audiences and evaluation criteria for their work.

Topic selection is an important task for students in this stage. To do research well, the students have to be knowledgeable about the topic and the topic has to be an appropriate level of abstraction.

> **Having a good understanding of the topic will allow the students to develop research questions or categories for investigation.**

Young researchers (i.e., 5 to 11 year olds) or inexperienced researchers of any age are more able to handle general knowledge topics where the emphasis is on fact-finding and organization of ideas. Junior high or middle school students (i.e., 12 to 15 year olds) are just beginning to be able to handle the abstract reasoning involved in focussing or narrowing a topic or for developing a position paper (Loerke, 1994). High school students (i.e., 16 to 18 year olds) can develop and support a thesis statement if they have had good research experience in earlier years.

Teachers generally will have planned the assignment and its parameters long before the students begin their work on the assignment.

> **Teachers should be looking for topics that students will find personally compelling and that students can connect to the out-of-school world (Tallman, 1998).**

For complex topics or for assignments where students are given wide choices, this means a repeat or cycling of the first two stages of the information literacy process so that students have the opportunity to do general reading, to assess sources of information, and to develop their interest and focus. Many information literacy process models give little attention to the complexity of this initial stage (Anderson, 1994).

> **Careful and thoughtful work is needed here to ensure that topics and research questions require high level thinking skills that will challenge students and engage their interest and curiosity.**

Students feel more positive towards investigative activities when they are involved in choosing or developing research topics; unfortunately there is some evidence that students in the senior grades may have less involvement in topic and question generation than do younger students (Gross, 1997).

Stage 2: Locating

In the Locating stage, students obtain the sources of information needed. If students are young or inexperienced, or if information on the topic is very hard to access, a stations approach, organizing the materials by format or media, is often effective.

> *Knowledge of information tools and systems and of search strategies (source and pathfinder approaches) is critical if the students are finding their sources independently.*

Students may experience information overload during the Locating stage (Akin, 1998). Teachers should be alert to the feelings and physical outlets that may characterize information overload - anger, frustration, fatigue, irritability, leg jiggling or swearing - and help students to recognize these signs of overload. In addition to helping students understand that such feelings are not an unusual part of the information literacy process, teachers should help students to identify useful strategies such as omission or filtering (ignoring or selecting certain categories of information), generalizing or twigging (broadening or narrowing the topic), or asking for help.

Whole class or small group activities related to getting a large picture of the topic and its sub-categories, such as concept-mapping, or deciding what kinds of information might be appropriate for the topic are helpful strategies for the Locating stage, especially when information overload is a problem.

Stage 3: Selecting/Analysing

In the Selecting/Analysing stage, students select and record information pertinent to their topic. Here is where the time invested in the Defining stage pays off; students who do not have a clear understanding of their topic (a topic focus) cannot select pertinent information. The Selecting/Analysing stage should involve a search for pertinent information, for information that will answer the students' questions or fit into their subtopics, not writing down everything they can find.

> **This is often where electronic resources or the photocopy machine can actually be a detriment to the process.**

For recording information, many students will need to be helped to take notes in some format. The format should be provided for inexperienced researchers.

Stage 4: Organising/Synthesising

In this stage, the students organize and synthesize their information in a unique and personal way.

> **Having students talk before writing can help them express their ideas in their own words.**

The students categorize information according to various frameworks, developed by them or provided for them, such as time order or cause and effect. The students look for inconsistencies or deficiencies in their information and locate information to rectify such problems.

Stage 5: Creating/Presenting

In the Creating/Presenting stage, the students create a research product.

Many information literacy models are somewhat biased toward the written report, but other media such as charts and multimedia productions also need revision (and instruction if the media is new to the student). They then present the research product in a way that is meaningful for a particular audience. There is also opportunity for the students to consider the role of the audience members in enhancing the sharing experience.

> *The audience, preferably a wider audience than just the teacher, should have been identified in the Defining stage so that the shaping of the sharing mode is possible.*

For young or inexperienced researchers, small group sharing is often more successful and more time efficient than sharing with the whole class.

Stage 6: Evaluating

In the Evaluation stage, the emphasis is on involving the students in the assessment of the process as well as the product of the research. The emphasis may at times be on assessing the students' understanding of the process or of the content. Evaluation need not be summative.

> *Some of the worst abuses of research as a learning experience grow out of an emphasis on creating the product; with the focus on the final product, students may simply become more skilful in plagiarizing (McGregor, 1995).*

Assessing the process may take the form of students creating a flow chart of the information literacy process.

Another alternative is having students prepare a written or oral summary of what they have learned about the process, or what content they have learned through the process.

Having middle grade students write a letter to their parents can be very effective way of having students identify and assess their own learning.

Students who are mentored in metacognitive awareness show growth in both content knowledge and search strategies.

Teaching the Information Literacy Process: Overall Themes

Developing emotional literacy

The information literacy process approach emphasizes the affective as well as cognitive aspects of the process. Students need to be helped to recognize as natural the waves of optimism and frustration that accompany complex learning (Kuhlthau, 1993).

Schroeder and Zarinnia (2001b) point out that, when information literacy programs utilize problem-based learning, emotional problems may increase since some students become anxious when facing problems that have no right answer, when the process of problem solving has only limited structure, and when multiple perspectives have to be taken into account.

Students need to be aware of, and have coping strategies, to address such challenges of problem based learning as well as such common phenomena as library anxiety and information overload.

The point here is not to try to have only positive feelings or to eliminate negative feelings but to recognize them as normal parts of learning, to understand them, and to regulate them.

Students who understand that their feelings are not unique but shared by others, are less likely to be overwhelmed by them.

Investing time in exploration

The problem solving emphasis of the information literacy process approach means a shift in the way we think about and use time. More time is needed in early stages of the process for exploration, for building content knowledge, for developing a personal interpretation or focus.

This is not a waste of time but time well invested in developing students' interest in and commitment to the topic being researched. Steeves (1994) found that even very young researchers in Grades 1 and 2, given the opportunity for lengthy and rich exploration of a topic, could develop a clear understanding of the information literacy process as well as producing unique and original research products.

Her young researchers, investigating Insect Life, spent almost half of their research time in this early exploration stage, reading and talking about insects, hearing stories and singing songs about insects, watching videos about insects and going on a "bug walk" in the school yard.

They were immersed in their topic, in ways that engaged both the affective and cognitive domains. Their interest and commitment to finding out about insects was deep enough to sustain them when they faced the challenges of finding answers to the questions that they had generated.

> *Garland (1995) found that older students were more interested in their research topics if they had solid background knowledge of the topic area and could see the purpose of the research and its connection to their other schoolwork.*

Supporting students during their work

The staged model of the information literacy process suggests that students might experience different feelings, thoughts, and actions at each stage. This also calls for different kinds of teacher and teacher-librarian involvement or mediation at the various stages in the process.

> *Teachers have found that students, who were taught using an information literacy process approach, where the investigative work was integrated with the curriculum, found the students became "more creative, more positive, more independent" (Kühne, 1995, p.25).*

This was true for poorer students as well as for the stronger students, although the poorer students needed more individual attention during the process. Todd (1995) has suggested that teachers and librarians think about their work with students as a conversation, an active interchange through which meaning is constructed. This interchange is discursive, adaptive, interactive and reflective. Students are encouraged to talk about their knowledge and teachers and librarians enter into this conversation with suggestions on how the student can move forward, see things from new perspective, make connections between previous and new knowledge, and see the patterns of their learning.

Teaching role of the librarian

Some librarians are reluctant to take an active teaching role in working with teaching colleagues in schools but, without taking up that teaching role, the new information literacy models are not likely to be implemented (Hazelwood, 1994).

An information literacy process model is difficult to implement fully even when there is a knowledgeable teacher-librarian and a school policy that supports the constructivist philosophy of learning that underpins the model.

> *However, teachers who have worked collaboratively with teacher-librarians were impressed by the creative and imaginative learning experiences that resulted from cooperative planning with teacher-librarians and thought teacher-librarians needed to be more assertive in inviting teachers to engage in cooperative planning (Sweeney, 1994).*

Understanding the process approach

Even teachers and teacher-librarians who are aware of the process models sometimes believe they are implementing their model but are actually leaving out the aspects that in fact, are critical to the success of the model. For example, in Canada, Holland (1994) found that teachers' implementation of the *Focus on Research* model was hampered by their limited understanding of the model, particularly in relation to the critical importance of reviewing the process with students.

A statement in the *Focus on Research* document suggesting that a research activity need not include all stages and skills seemed to have been taken to mean that important aspects of the model, such as involving students in the Defining stage to identify the question or problem that is to be addressed, and involving students in reviewing the cognitive and affective aspects of the information literacy process, could be omitted entirely.

In the United States, Tastad and Collins (1997) also found that implementing process approaches was difficult in schools where the teaching practices and curriculum did not support a process or constructivist approach.

Conclusion

Teaching the information literacy process in ways that respect the interests and needs of young people is a complex and fascinating educational task, one that demands the very best of our knowledge and skills as teachers and librarians. An enormous amount of research has been conducted over the past two decades that can contribute to this work with young people. The research on affect and its relation to learning is being done in both of the fields from which we draw the theories that guide our work in teaching the information literacy process, the fields of education and of library and information studies.

Affect involves pleasure, engagement, motivation, imagination, participation in community, and acknowledgement of other voices. These elements provide the energy that keeps young people engaged in inquiry-based and problem-based activities.

> *Absence of affective reward is a key element in alienation from learning and from schooling.*

We as teachers and as teacher-librarians need to keep abreast of this growing body of research and we need to use it to reflect upon and improve our practice on an ongoing basis.

> *Without a deep understanding of the process approach to information literacy, we are likely to continue traditional practices, some of which push learners to "get to work" too early and prevent them from developing a personal perspective and motivation for learning through investigation.*

References

Alberta Education. (1990). *Focus on Research: A guide to developing students' research skills.* Edmonton, Alberta: Author.

Akin, L. (1998). Information overload and children: A survey of Texas elementary school students. *SLMQ Online.* Available online: http://www.ala.org/aasl/SLMQ/overload.html, September 10, 1998.

American Association of School Librarians (AASL). (1999). Learning through the library. Available online: http://www.ala.org/aasl/learning/index.html, April 28, 1999.

Anderson, D. (1994). Seeking a clearer focus: Further considerations for teaching a research process. *School Libraries in Canada,* 14(3), 25-28.

Bush, G. (1998). Be true to your school: Real-life learning through the library media center. *Knowledge Quest,* 26(3), 28-31.

Flavell, J.F. (1979) Metacognition and cognitive monitoring. *American Psychologist,* 34(10), 906-911.

Garland, K. (1995). The information search process: A study of elements associated with meaningful research tasks. *School Libraries Worldwide,* 1(1), 41-53.

Gross, M. (1997). Pilot study on the prevalence of imposed inquiries in a school library media center. *School Library Media Quarterly,* 25(3), 157-166.

Harada, V. H. (1998). Building a professional community for student learning. *Knowledge Quest,* 26(3), 22-26.

Hazelwood, R. (1994). *Research assignments, the information search process, and resource use in a high school: A case study.* Unpublished master's thesis, University of Alberta, Edmonton, Canada.

Holland, S. (1994). *Working together to implement Focus on Research in a rural elementary classroom.* Unpublished master's thesis, University of Alberta Edmonton, Canada.

Kuhlthau, C. C. (1993). *Seeking meaning: A process approach to library and information services.* Norwood, NJ: Ablex.

Kühne, B. (1994). The Barkestorpe project: Investigating school library use. *School Libraries Worldwide*, 1(1), 13-27.

Loerke, K. (1992). Developing a focus in the research process. *Alberta Learning Resources Journal*, 11(2), 7-13.

Loerke, K. (1994). Teaching the library research process in junior high. *School Libraries in Canada*, 14(2), 23-26.

McGregor, J. H. (1994). An analysis of thinking in the research process. *School Libraries in Canada*, 14(2), 4-7.

McGregor, J. H. (1995). Process or product: Constructing or reproducing knowledge. *School Libraries Worldwide*, 1(1), 28-40.

Oberg, D. (1999). Teaching the research process—For discovery and personal growth. *Conference Proceedings of the 65th IFLA Conference and General Council*, held in Bangkok, Thailand, Booklet 3, pp. 52-60. Available online: http://www.ifla.org/IV/ifla65/papers/078-119e.htm

Ryan, J., & Capra, S. (2001a). Information literacy planning for educators: The ILPO approach. *School Libraries Worldwide*, 7(1), 1-10.

Ryan, J., & Capra, S. (2001b). *Information literacy toolkit, Grades Kindergarten-6.* Chicago: American Library Association.

Ryan, J., & Capra, S. (2001c). *Information literacy toolkit, Grades 7-12.* Chicago: American Library Association.

Schroeder, Elaine E., & Zarinnia, E. Anne. (2001a). Problem-based learning: Develop information literacy through real problems. *Knowledge Quest*, 30(1), 34-35.

Schroeder, Elaine E., & Zarinnia, E. Anne. (2001b). Problem-based learning: Developing information literacy through solving real world problems. *Paper presented at Treasure Mountain Research Retreat 9, Nashville, IN, November 13-14, 2001.*

Slavoney, P., & Sluyter, D.J. (1997). *Emotional development and emotional intelligence.* New York: Basic Books.

Steeves, P. (1994). Workshop for knowledge construction: A view of the research process in the elementary school. *School Libraries in Canada*, 14(2), 8-10.

Sweeney, L. (1994). *Collegial experiences: Teachers and teacher-librarians working together.* Unpublished master's thesis, University of Alberta, Edmonton, Canada.

Tallman, J. (1998). I-search: An inquiry-based, student centered, research and writing process. *Knowledge Quest*, 27(1), 20-27.

Tastad, S. A., & Collins, N. D. (1997). Teaching the information skills process and the writing process: Bridging the gap. *School Library Media Quarterly*, 25(3), 167-169.

Toben, J. (1997). A kaleidoscope view of change: Bringing emotional literacy into the library learning experience. *Knowledge Quest,* 26(1), 22-27.

Todd, R. J. (1995). Information literacy: Philosophy, principles, and practice. *School Libraries Worldwide*, 1(1), 54-68.

Can we prevent copying?
Transforming scribes into thinkers

Joy McGregor

The website has a catchy name: *School Sucks!* The shock value captures attention, capitalising on a commonly held belief of many students, that school does indeed *suck*.

The basic premise of this site is shared with many similar sites, i.e., that the educational system supports poor pedagogy …

> *…when teachers assign research paper topics so unoriginal that they can be reproduced and sold - or sometimes given away - to countless other students in other schools, other cities, other countries, who are required to complete the exact same assignment.*

(e.g., Evil House of Cheat, Absolutely Free: Online Essays, Cheater.com, Cheat Factory. For URLs, see end of document):

Users are cautioned on most of these sites not to plagiarise, since teachers are aware that the sites exist. The suggested use of the papers available for download is as research background or a trigger for ideas. While there could well be merit in these uses, and while the point of poor pedagogy may be well taken, the predominant use of papers from these sites is likely to be an easy solution to the problems of lack of time, procrastination, lack of ideas, or disinterest.

Many students who copy papers from sites like these, or who use other plagiarism techniques, probably feel inadequate in terms of their own ability to successfully write a worthy paper.

> *How did students reach a point where claiming someone else's work as their own became an acceptable solution?*

What students learn when they gather and use information might not be what they are expected to learn. Teachers and teacher librarians expect worthwhile outcomes when they assign research papers and projects that require searching for information and using that information to create a new document. Possible results might be these:

- gaining skill in locating information;

- dealing with ambiguity;

- analysing, evaluating, and synthesising information;

- organising thinking;

- developing a focus;

- relating similar ideas;

- learning new content; and

- developing new interests.

Packaging the newfound information into a final product such as a research paper could result in further outcomes:

- learning to organise information in a logical sequence; and

- learning to communicate ideas clearly in a commonly understood format.

But are these gains really made?

My experience as a teacher librarian made me doubt whether many of those outcomes were actually accomplished. It concerned me that I often saw little engagement in a topic and a lack of the necessary skills to carry out the assigned task. It seemed that students were learning to dread the task of using information, rather than improving their ability to do so effectively. This observation made me want to know more about the phenomenon, resulting in two research studies related to student information use.

The first study looked specifically at the kinds of thinking used by grade eleven students trying to use information. The data collected led to an examination of the process and/or product orientation of the students involved. While plagiarism was not originally under direct observation, the high degree of plagiarism could not be ignored and it led to a question of whether or not the tendency to plagiarise was related to the students' thinking in any way.

All students demonstrated a product orientation - a desire to create a good paper, a focus on the expected format - not an unexpected result. Some students, however, also showed an orientation to such processes as seeking meaning in the information they found, making sense of the ideas, learning about the topic, or understanding something new.

Process orientation showed in statements such as "I have to talk out my ideas in order to understand what I'm thinking", or "I almost think it's better this way, that we get to study about it in the first place and then formulate our own ideas and our own thoughts on it" and "It's a little harder to figure out what's going on when you have to figure it out for yourself, rather than have somebody tell you. I think it's more worthwhile, 'cause we'll learn it better" (student quotes).

> *The students who showed any process orientation did not plagiarise, while many of those who showed only product orientation tended to copy to a greater or lesser degree.*

They also demonstrated more complex analytical skills such as comparison, discovery of cause and effect, inference, prediction, and use of analogy, while the students who showed only product orientation demonstrated only categorising and sequencing as skills of analysis.

I conducted a second study to look more closely at the process/product orientation of students the same age and involved in a similar research paper task. These students received direct instruction about plagiarism and correct citation format, as well as constant reminders to cite all quotations and paraphrased ideas.

The teacher required three short quotations and one long one, to provide practice for correct citation, but students received no instruction on choosing quotations, deciding when or what to quote, or using them effectively within their own text.

Students received handouts with instructions on how to paraphrase and examples of good and poor paraphrasing, but few students identified these handouts as being useful. It appeared that the teacher and the students assumed that they understood the principle and technique of paraphrasing and did not need instruction on it. When asked how they paraphrase, most students described substituting occasional words with synonyms, rather than determining underlying ideas and thinking about what they meant and how they could be expressed in a way that was meaningful to the individual.

When adults are asked to paraphrase various quotations, they quickly identify the need to understand or make sense of the quotation before they can put it in their own words. Teachers and teacher librarians typically find Quotation A (below) much easier to paraphrase than Quotation B.

Quotation A

Somehow the natural, universal, or intuitive learning that takes place in one's home or immediate surroundings during the first years of life seems of an entirely different order from the school learning that is now required throughout the literate world. (Gardner, 1991: 2)

Quotation B

By showing its affinities with positivism, Roman's analysis has enabled us to be critical of those assumptions within naturalistic ethnography that affirm atomistic accounts of complex social realities and the intellectual tourism and voyeurism of researchers.
(Roman and Apple, 1990: 64)

They can identify many steps they must take in order to paraphrase Quotation B. Adults such as teachers and teacher librarians are probably closer to the expert end of the novice-to-expert spectrum than grade eleven students in being able to paraphrase. They describe thinking about the meaning of the sentence, relating it to personal experience, and determining how it fits into prior knowledge as steps they go through. When trying to paraphrase Quotation B, they describe being frustrated with not understanding the sentence, not being familiar with the vocabulary, not being able to relate it to prior knowledge, and not being interested in the topic.

> *Yet, students are often asked to put ideas into their own words, when they have no prior knowledge or information related to things they understand or care about.*

Adults readily recognise that paraphrasing is a complex, difficult skill. Through the previous exercise, they begin to realise the need for providing students with scaffolding to enable them to successfully carry out information use tasks such as paraphrasing.

> *Synthesis, too, is a complex skill, involving a need to seek meaning and make sense of information.*

When asked to synthesise information from two related, but somewhat differently focused, passages, adults realise the complexity of the task. They discover how involved their thinking must be - among other things, determining the meaning of each passage, finding a context in which both of them fit, comparing and contrasting ideas, determining which ideas can be related to one another and in what way, relating the original passages to prior knowledge, finding a focus to which both passages can be directed, and thinking critically about the concepts involved.

> *At what point do students gain practice at these skills and techniques?*

When do they become aware that skills like paraphrasing and synthesising are complex, but doable? What help do they receive to strengthen their abilities in these areas? All too often these skills are assumed or only taught cursorily.

The papers in the second study were analysed for the way in which students scribed (McGregor and Streitenberger, 1998).

> **Scribing can be described as "incorporating someone else's words into a product, either legitimately, by quoting and citing, or illegitimately, by copying".**

Scribing was extensive - each paper contained at least 20% and up to 95% scribing. Since students were required to provide a minimum number of quotations, it is understandable that the lowest amount of scribing was 20%, but when 85% of the students scribed at least half their papers, the question emerges as to how much of the material scribed is actually understood and how much is simply inserted to fulfil requirements.

Students plagiarised considerably less in the second study than students in the first study. The warnings about plagiarism by their teacher probably paid off. Perhaps the fact that she required them to take all their notes by copying word for word and then handing in their notes along with their final papers made them uneasy about copying. Perhaps they really developed an understanding of the necessity to try to quote properly or paraphrase.

But further analysis of their quotations yielded information about the kinds of copying/quoting/scribing they did. While all students quoted at least 20% of their papers, many scribed much larger portions of their papers. The type of errors in citation and quotation seemed to indicate an attempt to make the citations look right, even though the attempts were often filled with inaccuracy.

Piaget studied students' errors to determine whether error patterns could tell him anything about their thinking. Following this line of thinking, students in this study quoted the wrong sources, combined quotes from multiple sources and then cited completely different ones, and copied the quotes incorrectly in many cases.

> **Appearances seemed to be the key - "if it looks right, it's good enough" seemed to be the modus operandi.**

- How much thinking goes on in situations like this?

- Are students learning what we hope they will learn?

- Do students really understand the portions they scribe?

- How much of that information is incorporated into their mental models of the topic, becoming part of their own knowledge?

- Or is the product orientation - making it look good - the driving force, with little else going on intellectually?

> **Computer programs use the cloze technique to detect plagiarism.**

The basic premise in the software is that students who composed their own sentences and paragraphs are more likely to be able to fill in missing words than students who plagiarised. The research behind these computer programs supports the idea that students who plagiarise aren't as likely to learn (Glatt, 1987). Perhaps this conclusion can be extended to students who scribe extensive portions of their papers. Students who copy more than half their paper from an original source (as 85% of those in the second study did), whether they cite the quotations correctly or not, may not be constructing much new knowledge.

> **Those students, who synthesise the ideas, incorporating them into a basic premise of their own making, are very likely learning more than their scribing counterparts.**

Can this situation be changed? No long lasting or permanent change will occur as long as teachers and teacher librarians ignore the copying they know is going on.

Responsibility for teaching children to work with ideas and incorporate them into their own mental models through synthesis must be shared among educators from primary to adult levels of education.

> **What strategies could make a difference to the amount and depth of understanding that students develop?**

- A change in the nature of assignments requiring information use. Students in the first study used more complex analytical skills when the topic required critical thinking.

- Providing challenging questions that intrigue students, to generate more interest and promote a desire to think and learn, rather than to regurgitate.

- Active learning projects that involve students in knowledge construction rather than reproduction of other people's ideas.

- Direct instruction on skills such as paraphrasing and synthesising, providing students with tools for tackling these complex tasks.

- Encouraging students at an early age to summarise ideas that they hear, rather than only those that they read.

- Summarising the main points after a discussion provides practice in putting thoughts into words without actually seeing the words in print first.

- Giving students the opportunity to talk about the information they find, possibly to an adult (teacher or teacher librarian), to peers, or to themselves through reflection. Conversation allows them the opportunity to explore the relevance of the ideas to their own use in the immediate situation.

- Keeping research journals or writing logs to help students develop and construct their thoughts and identify the gaps in their thinking.

- Encouraging metacognition (thinking about thinking) on a regular basis. Direct emphasis on metacognition builds good thinking habits awareness that thinking is taking place.

Transforming scribes into thinkers will not be an easy task, but students who are encouraged to be active learners and critical and reflective thinkers will be better educated in the end.

> *The less the act of scribing is reinforced, and the more students are encouraged to construct their own knowledge, the more effectively information use will promote learning.*

Sample 'model' paper websites

A-1 term paper academic and business research source. (Online).
www.a1-termpaper.com

Absolutely free online essays. (Online).
www.ee.calpoly.edu~ercarlso/papers.htm

The evil house of cheat. (Online).   www.CheatHouse.com

The paper store. (Online).   www.termpapers-on-file.com

School sucks. (Online).   schoolsucks.com

References

Glatt, B. (1987). *The cognitive consequences of parroting.* Ed.D. diss.,
    University of Chicago.

Gardner, H. (1991). *The unschooled mind.* New York: Basic Books.

McGregor, J.H. and Streitenberger, D. (1998). Do scribes learn?
    Copying and information use. *SLMQ Online.* (Online). Retrieved
    July 11, 1999.   www.ala.org/aasl/SLMQ/scribes.html

Roman, L.G. and Apple, M.W. (1990). Is naturalism a move away from
    positivism? In E.W. Eisner and A. Peshkin (eds.) *Qualitative
    inquiry in education.* New York: Teachers College Press.

Critical literacy: a building block towards the information literate school community

Linda Langford

Preamble

In my paper entitled *Information literacy: seeking clarification* (Langford, 1999), I grapple with semantics. This came as a result of my frustration over a concept that was being bandied around, written into school's mission and vision statements and being toted as the teacher librarian's core business. It was frustrating because, depending on what end of the elephant you had in your grasp, informed your understanding of this concept.

I was able to tease out a number of literacies that were being generated as fast as I could read the literature on literacy or digest what research was available. Critical literacy was one aspect that I had included in my map of information literacy (ibid: 49). It was grouped with ethical, moral, and information problem-solving literacies. Today, I question what critical literacy is about and how we develop this literacy.

In a global society endeavouring to make sense of the information surrounding us, critical literacy has proved to be a difficult concept. Misson (1998) posits the definition that critical literacy is both process and practice and that it centres on making clear new ideologies and the consequent ideological working of texts. Certainly the struggle between the existing model of Industrial Age schools with the demands of a Communication Age society begs that we come to some pedagogical grip with a literacy that finds its challenge in emerging communication technologies.

If we are serious about the new teaching and learning paradigm that is emerging as a consequence of the *Net Education System* so aptly coined by Mal Lee (1999), then critical literacy must lie in a learning culture that is informed by a conceptual understanding of information literacy.

> **As a society, we are evermore conscious of the need to be continuously learning, to keep developing as information literate human beings.**

The development of the skills and practices of critical literacy are more vital than ever to school curricula. How will schools take on this challenge? Can they emerge as information literate school communities?

I believe that Industrial Age schooling must crumble and give rise to a more student-centred, goal-oriented, caring environment, which fosters active involvement, and risk taking, and ongoing personal mastery. This paper supports the thesis that critical literacy, as a subset of information literacy, relies on the development of critical and creative thinking within the information process: the scaffold for continuous learning.

Critical literacy: possible understandings

> **Critical literacy has as many points of view as information literacy. It is my thesis that critical literacy is but one literacy that combines with other literacies to develop a continually inquiring human mind.**

One never becomes critically literate because one never becomes information literate (Langford, 1999; Henri, 1999)! The continuum is dynamic and centres on our continuous learning if we are to be effective and creative beings, able to relate and reassess the ideological workings in a text... from an advertising flyer to an economic/political initiative like GST. As a concept, it can be manifested in an aspect of the information process, that is, the development of thinking.

> **The information environment, tied to emerging technologies, forces us to adopt a manner of continuous learning in order to function well in society at whatever point in time, using whatever skills we have developed, to make sense of an ever-changing information climate. (Buckland, 1991).**

Critical literacy is but one building block towards this societal imperative to make sense of all that seeks to inform.

Critical literacy could be defined as 'taking the learner beyond thoughtful reflection to analysis and a determined course of action' (Jones 1996). Within a conceptual view of information literacy, a view that perceives learning as a series of multiple arrivals along a continuous journey, critical literacy's foci rests on the developing skills of thinking.

To develop critical literacy, that is our ability to recast our thinking through metacognitive processes (Paul, 1993; McGregor, 1999), we may need to experience, adopt, and apply a degree of skills and attitudes that free us to recast our thinking.

These skills and attitudes would enable us to shift our mental models of *what is...to... what can be* as we hone the skills necessary to differentiate between fact and opinion, examining extrinsic and intrinsic assumptions, remaining focussed on the big picture whilst examining the specifics. Awareness of fallacious arguments, ambiguity and manipulative reasoning (Jones, 1996) coupled with flexibility and open mindedness would contribute to a state of deep critical thinking.

Critical and creative thinking: sustaining critical literacy

Analysing the work of academics like Jones, McGregor, Paul, Todd and Meyers, provides a good base for developing identifiers of critical and creative thinkers.

> *These identifiers have significantly extended the concept of critical literacy, as understood by those who coined the term, as the 'use of language in all of its forms, as in thinking, solving problems, or communicating' (Venezky, 1982).*

These identifiers support the notion of critical literacy as a set of processes centering on the development of thinking.

The following set of features (Jones, 1996) serves to identify some of the characteristics that may define a critically literate community:

- can approach something new in a logical manner;
- can look at how others have approached the same question or problem, but know when they need more information;
- can use creative and diverse ways to generate a hypothesis, approach a problem or answer a question;
- can take their critical thinking skills and apply them to everyday life;
- can clarify assumptions, and recognise that they have causes and consequences;
- can support their opinions with evidence, data, logical reasoning, and statistical measures;
- can look at a problem from multiple angles;
- can not only fit the problem within a larger context, but decide if and where it fits in the larger context;
- are comfortable with ambiguity.

Further to this list, the CTILAC Advisory Board (1998,1999) adds that critical and creative thinking implies that there is purpose to the thinking, that is, that there is an information problem to be solved. Therefore this would call upon the skills inherent in analysis, synthesis and evaluation.

They add weight to Jones' (1996) summation by pointing out that critical and creative thinkers recognise:

- patterns and provide a way to use those patterns to solve a problem or answer a question;

- errors in logic, reasoning, or the thought process;

- what is irrelevant or extraneous information;

- preconceptions, bias, values and the way that these affect our thinking;

- that these preconceptions and values mean that any inferences are within a certain context;

- ambiguity - that there may be more than one solution or more than one way to solve a problem.

> *Does critical literacy therefore have a relational role to critical and creative thinking? Can critical literacy be the platform for a whole school curriculum?*

And if so, can this whole school approach translate to an information literate school community: a learning community that is in the business of 'continually creating its future' (Senge 1992)?

Critical literacy: beyond rhetoric in education

Perhaps a more useable perspective for schools might be in viewing critical literacy as interpreting the intellectual and social value of information (Buckland, 1991; Langford, 1999: 49). This then would call up the higher order thinking skills that lead to decision-making, creating, and synthesising the outcomes of the myriad forms of literacy.

If critical literacy can develop from a metacognitive approach to recognising the need to think critically and creatively, then the *skills* involved can be developed. It is especially pertinent that educators appreciate that critical literacy, which has as its twin skill sets critical and creative thinking, is not a set of sectoralised skills reserved for say, the English classroom, but is a shared set of skills across all disciplines.

As Meyers (1995) so clearly delineates:

- critical thinking is a learnable skill with teachers and peers serving as resources;

- problems, questions, and issues serve as the source of motivation for the learner;

- courses are assignment centred rather than text or lecture oriented.

- goals, methods, and evaluation emphasise using content rather than simply acquiring it;

- students need to formulate and justify their ideas in writing;

- students collaborate to learn and enhance their thinking.

> *If we agree that critical literacy emphasises mental attitudes or dispositions and the concomitant application of reasoning to everyday situations, then we might argue that the building blocks of analysis, synthesis, and evaluation are the building blocks that develop critical literacy.*

How we apply those building blocks will determine the extent of our critical and creative thinking (McGregor, 1999). No matter how we view the building blocks, we must be conscious that literate practice is always morally and politically loaded; and that our world view stems from our ability to 'render explicit the belief systems inscribed in the text, and so negate their power' (Misson, 1998: 11). We must also be conscious that critical literacy be a shared understanding if it is, as it should be, a foundation to sound education.

Critically literate: the learning community

However we view critical literacy, it must centre on thought and our belief that, through developing the processes of thinking, our attitudes will be shaped. Our values and beliefs, coupled with the ability to solve problems, are partners in developing and shaping our world-view. And this sharpening and developing of our world-view critically asks us to appraise our information environment... to assess the *chingdou* (Handy, 1997) as we seek meaning.

A highly critically literate learning community acts through an *unconscious consciousness,* aware only that the determined course of action takes the group onward towards successful outcomes, towards functioning well in society. The processes and practices that inform critical literacy, that is the *tools of truth making,* are well honed.

> *The capacity to think about their thinking, analyse and apply thought, create knowledge and act will reflect the quality of that learning community; the quality of that information literate school community.*

Back to school

Information literacy, as seen from a holistic platform, is perceived within a journey of multiple arrivals, connecting to the continuous honing of our mental capacities: our critical literacy, our technological literacy, our cultural literacy, and our functional literacy! Let us not argue about the nature of information literacy anymore.

Let us accept that we must move beyond the jargon of learning how to learn and critically examine and synthesise the connecting aspects of the information literacy map (Langford, 1999) as teachers and as teacher librarians. Let us reconstruct our understanding of an information literate school community.

Let us acknowledge a paradigm shift from information skills thinking to lifelong learning thinking, complete with the metacognitive skills of critical literacy: critical and creative thinking. Let us truly set our young people onward towards the goal of functioning well in society.

My belief is that this is a far more regenerative concept for educators to be a part of than some narrowly defined information literacy concept.

The truth is out there!

References

Buckland, M. (1991). Information as thing. *Journal of the American Society for Information Science.* 42(5): 351-360.

CTILAC Advisory Board. Critical Thinking Definition (1998, 1999). (online). http://ir.bcc.ctc.edu/library/ilac/critdef.htm

Bellevue Community College. (online). < http://ir.bcc.ctc.edu/library/ilac/critdef.htm >

Handy, C. (1997). *The hungry spirit.* London: Hutchinson

Henri, J. (1999). "The information literate school community: not just a pretty face!" In Henri, J. and Bonanno, K. (eds.) *The information literate school community.* Wagga Wagga: Centre for Information Studies, Charles Sturt University: 4.

Jones, D. (1996). Critical thinking in an online world. (online) < http://www.library.ucsb.edu/untangle/jones.html#savery >

Langford, L. (1999). "Information literacy: seeking clarification". In Henri, J. and Bonanno, K. (eds.) *The information literate school community.* Charles Sturt University, Wagga Wagga: Centre for Information Studies.

Lee, M. (1999). A new global education system. *Access* 13 (2): 15-16

McGregor, J. (1999). *Critical literacy and the Internet.* From seminar May 26 1999 Charles Sturt University, Wagga Wagga

Meyers, C. (1985). *Teaching students to think critically.* San Francisco: Jossey Bass.

Misson, R. & Christie, F. (1998). *Literacy and schooling*. London: Routledge.

Paul, R. (1993). *Critical thinking: how to prepare students for a rapidly changing world.*

Senge P. (1992). *The fifth discipline: the art and practise of the learning organisation.* NY: Random House

Venezky, R. (1982). "Linguistics and/or reading or is applied linguistics a caveat emptor technology?" In Frawley, W (ed.) *Linguistics and literacy*. New York: Plenum Press, 269-283.

E-literacies and Cybraries

Cushla Kapitzke

Libraries are a kind of monumental writing,
a writing and reading space in stone. (Bolter, 1991, p. 101)

School libraries are places - and digital spaces - where text and technology, literacy and learning, converge in concentrated and often contradictory ways.

Historically, the role of librarians as archivists and custodians was to select, organize and distribute society's cultural and symbolic capital.

Like all sites of cultural labour, librarianship had a language that was specific to its professional procedures and practices. The "Dewey Decimal Classification System" and "Boolean logic" are examples of "librarian-speak" that long have baffled, and indeed alienated, many young people in their school libraries. Typical textual practices of libraries in the past included searching the card catalogue and "periodical indexes," locating materials via their "call numbers," skim reading, and note-taking, or more recently, note-making.

Yet, new technologies are changing both schools and the libraries that serve their information needs. Online technologies are eliding the boundaries that once existed between physical and virtual space, between school and society, and between printed text and electronic formats.

In turn, these shifts and transformations are reconfiguring the nature of literacy, and the concept of information literacy.

Libraries and New Technologies

In the latter half of the twentieth century, digitisation, the Internet and hypertext propelled information access and exchange into the era of cyberspace and the cyber library, or cybrary. Networked telecommunications and information technologies are transforming not only the physical space of libraries, but are also changing the literate and textual work that takes place in them (Ensor, 1997). Milestones in the technologization of libraries included the automation of the catalogue, the installation of OPACs, the introduction of electronic materials such as stand-alone CD-ROM indexes to which librarians only had access, the adoption of online information databases, and more recently the shift to library websites and web-based catalogues (WebPacs). In the current transitional stage, digital or hybrid libraries integrate traditional and online services. Remote access decreases the necessity of going physically to a school or university library for informational materials, or in the case of virtual libraries, is eliminated altogether.

Whilst still located in buildings, libraries are gradually transforming into de-materialized nodes of virtual, informational space that span oral, print and digital cultures. The cybrary is, then, an electronic gateway for clients located anywhere to access information located everywhere. Cybraries function as electronic "portals" to information services that are accessed just as easily from across the country as across the campus or the counter. Without entering the premises or speaking to a librarian, a computer terminal with Internet access enables students to check if a book is on the shelf, request a particular resource, view their loans record, and peruse the list of new accessions. They can read lecture notes, course reading lists, exam papers, and university handbooks. Postgraduate students and staff can request and receive journal articles via email. The library homepage has become an entry point for subject-specific databases, full-text e-journals, free downloads of certain software, and information about online and face-to-face information skills training.

Cybraries and new e-literacies

What does this transformation of the library mean for school students and teachers?

> *In the process of problem solving, researching,*
> *and preparing assignments for publication on the World Wide Web,*
> *students draw from a multiplicity*
> *of blended online literacies, or e-literacies.*

They might start by searching an online catalogue and the electronic databases to which the library subscribes. To locate and retrieve material from the Internet, they would need to understand the differential uses and search protocols of the many subject directories, search engines, and meta-indexes available to them. If using webpage design or presentation applications, students would download or print information, drag and drop text; insert backgrounds; create borders; and make hyperlinks to material in the document or to other files and websites. Many students today are highly skilled at technological literacies such as importing audio files of background music or interview material, and inserting video clips and electronically scanned photos and images from other print materials.

These tasks assume technological competence in the creation and navigation of nested folders and directories; and in the creation, saving, naming, and renaming of files. Depending upon the software used, publishing a webpage requires network literacy to understand the local area network (LAN) and the procedures for transferring files back and forth to the server. Students also need socio-ethical competence in codes of practice for using and publishing both print and electronic material. This includes knowledge of issues concerning copyright; plagiarism; the rights and responsibilities of system access and security; and the standard social conventions regarding defamatory, obscene, or offensive material.

Information literacy

The technologisation of language and text has generated new theories and models for explaining and "doing" literate work. Visual literacy, digital literacy, media literacy, network literacy, critical literacy, and multiliteracies are some of them. The library profession's response to the proliferation of information was to reconfigure the library skills instruction programs of the 1960s into a research framework called "information literacy" (California Media & Library Educators Assoc., 1997). Most of the information science literature presents information literacy as an emerging framework rather than a fully defined, prescriptive model. Indeed, much of the literature bewails the slipperiness of the term and the lack of a universal definition with elaborated instructional goals and methods. Information literacy is variously understood as a process, a skill, or a competence. (For some definitions, see http://www.ucalgary.ca/library/ILG/litdef.html). Whilst it remains a highly contested term, two points upon which the profession agree are that information literacy should not be the domain of the teacher librarian alone, and that training around and about it should be integrated across all subject areas.

> *As used by librarians and teachers in Australia,*
> *information literacy comprises a hierarchy*
> *of information problem-solving skills*
> *that enable independent and effective learning.*

Most information literacy programs focus on tasks such as the creation and transmission of information, the construction and application of a search strategy, access to information (reference sources and periodical indexes), the structures of information (e.g., subject headings and the arrangement of database records), the physical organization of knowledge (e.g., the Dewey Decimal Classification System), and the evaluation of information.

One leading model espouses information literacy as a process of six steps. These are to: define an information task or problem, select appropriate resources, solve the problem, locate the resources, read or view the materials, synthesize the information, and evaluate the product and the problem-solving process (Eisenberg, 1996).

Yet, this process and these strategies have been appraised and found wanting for learning and working in the information economies and cultures of New Times (Luke & Kapitzke, 2000).

> **Whilst the ability to use and manipulate information is necessary, it is no longer sufficient.**

Students today need more than an understanding of the differences between "data, information and knowledge", and between "fact" and "fiction" because the non-linearity of hypertext is fast obliterating conventional categories of knowledge and its hierarchical organization in, for example, the Dewey Decimal System. Furthermore, the ephemeral and hybridised nature of digital environments tends to elide differences between real and virtual worlds, and therefore between factual and fictional ones.

> **Information literacy derives from a print-based culture.**

Its logic therefore maintains distinctions between fiction and non-fiction, and between reading for pleasure and reading for information. These distinctions and their associated practices such as the reading of novels in time reserved for 'silent, sustained reading' (SSR) are becoming increasingly obsolete and discriminatory. For many youth today, particularly in advanced capitalist countries like Australia, reading is no longer performed alone with a book. Rather, it is a shared activity undertaken with and around a computer screen while engaged in conversation with others who are in the room, in cyberspace, or in both (Tapscott, 1998).

Libraries are affected not only by technological change, but also by social and cultural change. Considering the important role played by information literacy in the educational enterprise, information literacy proponents should be mindful of the recent critical turn in educational theory and practice.

> **This entails moving information literacy from the confines of the library to the arenas of language use and the social lives of youth, which, in advanced economies, comprise wall-to-wall, multimodal ideas and information.**

It requires a sociology of information to account for the material and political bases of language and text use in libraries and their programs. As social practices, all literacies and e-literacies — including information literacy — are situated responses to specific educational contexts and classroom settings (Luke, 2000). Because the discursive and material resources framing library practices vary within and across institutional sites, so do their learning outcomes. Selective traditions of information usage comprising combinations of canons, genres, texts, literacy events, and social relations generate specific outcomes for certain social groups. Furthermore, those traditions of use confer differential identities, positions, functions, and powers to individuals in proportion to their mastery of the languages and discourses valorised by the literate economy in which they operate. Different library contexts instantiate different regimes of rules, rationales, procedures, and practices for textual work, which in turn are socially productive or counterproductive in terms of employment options and life chances for particular groups of students.

> **Information literacy is not solely about neutral cognitive processes or analytical thinking, but is about improving student opportunity and capacity to design and forge lifeworlds in a range of text-based communities.**

It may be a process and a skill, but viewing it also as a social construct and practice, opens a space for the possibility of social transformation through the interrogation and disruption of discourses that produce and reproduce social structures and economies, which are frequently inequitable.

> *Librarians, cybrarians, and teachers need therefore to shift their focus from a single, dominant theory of information literacy to the social and cultural construction of its pedagogies, and their variable political and discursive outcomes.*

A critical information literacy

> *This kind of critical information curriculum and pedagogy reframes conventional notions of text, knowledge, and authority, and in the process changes the traditional roles of students, teachers, and librarians.*

The library was the place students visited to acquire a selective tradition of information use and its application to a curricular unit. By contrast, the cybrary must be both a place and a space not only for learning information, but also for learning how to use information (i.e., the operational dimension such as using online databases), for learning about information (i.e., the critical and political dimension), and for learning through information (i.e., the cultural dimension) (cf., Lankshear, Snyder & Green, 2000).

Cybrarians, for example, can coordinate print and electronic resources between and among subject areas. With their expertise in the new information technologies and their knowledge of the collection, cybrarians can suggest texts that re/present a range of theoretical, ideological, and political perspectives on particular issues. Take, for example, the topic, globalisation.

Rather than seek the "facts" or the "truth" about its negative or positive impacts, student reading and research could focus on the social construction of the discourses and practices of economic and cultural integration, which have costs and benefits, advantages and drawbacks, in specific local and global contexts. In collaboration with the teacher, the cybrarian would furnish print and electronic texts produced by unionists, transnational corporations, indigenous peoples, feminists, environmentalists, and the World Trade Organisation, all of which present different and often conflicting versions of "reality."

> *Opportunity to analyse how these positions are materialized in language and text would show students that the production of knowledge necessarily entails relations of power that are able to be contested and transformed.*

Considering the power of information networks to connect and disconnect, include and exclude (Castells, 1996), any pedagogy that ignores the political economy of information does a disservice to students, irrespective of whether they are part of and contributing to, or disconnected from, the electronic current of the Communication Age.

Note: The content of this chapter is based on an article published in the *Journal of Adolescent and Adult Literacy*, 2001, 44(5), 450-456.

References

Bolter, J. D. (1991). *Writing space: The computer, hypertext, and the history of writing*. Hillsdale, NJ: Erlbaum.

California Media and Library Educators Assn. (1997). *From library skills to information literacy: A handbook from the 21st Century* (2nd ed.). Sacramento, CA: California School Library Association.

Castells, M. (1996). *The rise of the network society*. Oxford: Blackwell.

Ensor, P. (1997). *The cybrarian's manual*. Chicago: American Library Association.

Lankshear, C., Snyder, I., & Green, B. (2000). *Teachers and technoliteracy: Managing literacy, technology and learning in schools*. St Leonards, NSW: Allen & Unwin.

Luke, A. (2000). Critical literacy in Australia: A matter of context and standpoint. *Journal of Adolescent and Adult Literacy, 43*(5), 448-461.

Luke, A., & Kapitzke, C. (2000). Literacies and Libraries - Archives and Cybraries. *Curriculum Studies, 7*(3), 467-491.

Tapscottt, D. (1998). *Growing up digital: The rise of the Net generation*. New York: McGraw-Hill.

Literacy Webpages

http://www.edna.edu.au/EdNA/   — EdNA Online: Education Network Australia — government funded gateway for Australian educational resources.

http://www.hi.is/~anne/iasl.html   — webpage for the International Association for School Librarianship.

http://www.infolit.org/ — National Forum on Information Literacy — a coalition of over 75 education, business, and governmental organizations working to promote awareness of the need for information literacy and encouraging activities leading to its acquisition. Provides definitions of information literacy, descriptions of successful information literacy programs, and an extensive, annotated compendium of linked web sites.

Glossary

Boolean logic — a form of logic developed by the English mathematician, George Boole, which allows a database searcher to combine concepts in a keywords search using three commands or "operators": AND, OR, NOT.

Call number — a unique code displayed on the spine of library materials that represents the item in the library catalogue, and allows the user to locate the resource on the shelf.

Copyright — the exclusive legal right granted by government to an author, editor, composer, playwright, publisher, or distributor to publish, produce, sell, or distribute a literary, musical, dramatic, or artistic work. Copyright law also governs the right to prepare derivative works, to reproduce a work or portions of it, and to display or perform a work in public.

Cybrary — a cyber library is an electronic gateway or portal for clients physically located anywhere to access information located everywhere.

Dewey Decimal Classification System (DDC) — a system of classifying books and other works first published in 1876 by the librarian, Melvil Dewey, who divided human knowledge into ten basic categories with subdivisions indicated by decimal notation.

Discourse — recurring statements that constitute material and social relations of power.

Hybrid library — a library in which a significant proportion of the resources are available in digital format, as opposed to print or microform.

Information science — a branch of knowledge that investigates the sources, development, dissemination, use, and management of information in all its forms.

Online catalogue — a library catalogue consisting of bibliographic records in digital format maintained on a dedicated computer that provides uninterrupted access via workstations that are in direct, continuous communication with the central computer during each transaction.

Online services — the branch of library services concerned with selecting and providing access to electronic resources such as online databases and CD-ROMs, including mediated searching, which is usually handled by an online services librarian.

OPAC — Online Public Access Catalogue, a computer catalogue of the materials in a library.

Virtual library — a "library without walls" in which the collection and resources are accessible only electronically, and are not kept in paper, microform, or any tangible form.

WebPac — a public access online catalogue with a graphical user interface (GUI) accessible via the World Wide Web, as opposed to a text-based catalogue interface accessible via Telnet.
(Glossary adapted from Reitz, 2000).

Facilitating Problem-based Learning

Donald R Woods

Whether you are a tutor for a small group or a single instructor facilitating the PBL (Problem-based Learning) approach with classes of 20 to 80 students at once, the same attitude toward facilitation skills is needed.

Instructors or lecturers, by their very name, see their role primarily as lecturing. They stand and deliver. They do their own thing and try to facilitate learning. However, in PBL the instructor's role is to facilitate. The instructor is a coach. The coach does not do his/her own thing. The coach tries to bring out the best in the group.

In PBL the coach or facilitator brings out the best from the group by:

- asking leading and open-ended questions, to help the students explore the richness of the situation and to help them develop their critical thinking.

- helping students reflect on the experiences they are having, because reflection develops professional skill (Schon, 1987); reflection improves problem solving (Kimbell et al., 1991) and elaboration and reflection improves the learning (Schmidt, 1983; Coles, 1991). These reflective skills are part of effective problem solving and group skills.

- monitoring progress, because successful problem solvers monitor their thought processes about once per minute to ensure that they are still on track and that they understand where they are in the process (Schoenfeld, 1984). Monitoring is a key component in effective problem solving.

- challenging their thinking, so as to nurture deep learning and a search for meaning, and so that they develop their critical thinking skills.

- raising issues that need to be considered, because groups without facilitators tend to identify about 60% of the teacher's intended goals (Dolmans et al., 1993).

- stimulating, encouraging and creating and maintaining a warm, safe atmosphere in which individuals will be willing to share experiences and ideas without fear of being ridiculed, because trust is the key ingredient to develop (Covey, 1989). Such an environment nurtures trust.

All of these interventions address the process skills needed - skill in problem solving, critical thinking, group process, change management and lifetime learning.

The facilitator is not the group's expert resource who will provide the answers, nor should the facilitator use this as a chance to lecture. One might think that the best facilitator would be a non-expert in the discipline subject under consideration. However, such a facilitator is not sure when the students are off-base, or if they have misinterpreted the information. This is detrimental to the student's learning and to the facilitator's morale. If you feel unsure about the new role, you could try being a facilitator in someone else's class with that person present to keep the discussion on track "technically".

Why is the facilitative role vital?

Think of a newly-formed basketball team. Each member might be very skilled. But, guidance is needed to develop trust, help individuals to see their contributions, to provide perspective, to encourage and to critique. The coaching role is vital.

But how do we do this if we are a tutor? or if we are an instructor with 20 tutorless groups?

Being a tutor in a tutored group

Barrows and Tamblyn (1980), Sparks (1984) and Woods (1996) suggest the following comments that a facilitator might use:

- Hmmm, or other such acknowledging noises.

- I'm not sure that I follow you, would you mind repeating that so that I can understand your approach?

- Let's collect ideas about this.

- Any other ideas?

- Are you sure? Can you check that?

- Why is that? How come?

- Why did you come to that conclusion?

- Do you agree with what was just said?

- If what you suggest is true, then how would you explain...

- For this situation, have you ever considered or thought about...

- Are you sure of what you are saying?

- You seem unsure. Where could we find the information that would help you clarify this? Are there other ways to examine this problem? What are the assumptions being made? major? minor? hidden? flexible? questionable?

- Do you feel you need to look up that point?

- Why did you study this? Why was this work done? Why in this context?

- How is this related to other information? Are there inconsistencies? How can they be reconciled?

- What are some concrete examples?

- So what? What can we do now that we couldn't do before?

- Where does the new information lead?

In addition, the tutor can remind the participants of the importance of feedback, reflection and elaboration so as to improve learning.

The facilitator might ask:
- "Who is the chairperson for today's session? Who will be chairperson for the next session?"

- "Before we wrap up this session, might it be a good idea to reflect on how we handled the processing skills? For example, how well did we handle the problem solving dimensions? How did we function as a group? What were our five strengths and the two areas to work on? Can we set goals to improve our process skills for our next meeting?"

- "Do you wish to use feedback forms to guide what went on today? feedback for problem solving? for group process? for managing change? for chairperson? for self-directed, interdependent learning? for self-assessment?"

Naturally, which questions are asked and how the tutors fulfil their roles depends on how you have agreed to work. You should be comfortable with the role.

As a resident expert, the facilitator should respond to direct inquiries only when she/he is sure that the students have exhausted their own logic and that there is no other profitable learning experience for the students. The tutor's interjection should not rob the students of intellectual growth.

We could polish up our skills at facilitation, and those of our students, with the use of the Whimbey Pair Awareness activity.

The role of the "listener " in the Whimbey Pair Method is similar to the role of a "facilitator". For more about the Whimbey Pair Method, see D.R. Woods, PS News 36 (1985) and D.R. Woods, "PS Corner", Journal of College Science Teaching, 13, May, 469-472 (1984).

LuAnn Wilkerson (1994) has summarized feedback about student's expectation of the tutor in the context of PBL with a tutor available for each group. She identified seven, important facilitation skills. The students rated the excellence of the tutor, made anecdotal comments about what makes an excellent tutor and ranked the importance of the seven facilitation skills.

The codes for the skills are given in the footnote in Table 2.1. These skills are correlated with the ratings of the tutor (in column two of Table 2.1); enriched by the anecdotal comments (in column three of Table 2.1); and ranked by importance (in column four of Table 2.1). The responses of both the students and the tutors are included.

One of the main findings is that the "tutor must be willing to encourage student-directed discussion and value the development of both knowledge and skills in critical thinking."

	Statistically significant facilitation skills correlated with the "excellence of the tutor"		Facilitation skills included more frequently in the anecdotal comments for "excellent tutors".	Ranking of the "importance" of facilitator skills.
Student response	1*, 2,3,4 [accounts for 48% of the variance]	5,6 [33%]	1. Facilitates the task of the group process. 2. Guides the acquisition of subject knowledge. 3. Facilitates the morale components of the group process. 4. Stimulates critical analysis.	3,2,4,6 7,5,1
Tutor response	2,4,3 [52%]	5,6,1 [48%]		2,3,5, 6 7,5,4

Table 2.1: What students expect from their tutors in tutored groups
(from Wilkerson, 1994)

* Coded facilitation skills
  1. Provides frequent feedback.

  2. Questions and probes your reasoning process.

  3. Encourages critical appraisal of information.

  4. Helps students to balance basic science and clinical applications in problem discussion

  5. Encourages student direction of the tutorials

  6. Facilitates and supports good interpersonal relationships in the group.

  7. Promotes synthesis of multidisciplinary perspectives.

Clearly, many skills are needed simultaneously in small group, self-directed PBL - feedback, task and morale group processing skills, guidance with the subject.

- Knowledge (to keep students on track) and problem solving/critical reasoning skills.

- If we don't train and empower the students with these process skills, then they look to the tutor to provide them.

- Students enjoy being empowered to have student-centred discussion (compared with tutor-led discussion).

- Feedback (the * in the table with a factor loading of 0.932) is valued by the students and related to the excellence of the tutor. Without trying to read too much into these data, I suggest that the students are continually searching for feedback as to "how well am I learning the subject matter? Am I learning the right stuff? Am I learning it in sufficient depth?". Without such feedback, I think their stress level increases and the uncertainty undermines their performance.

So what? We see that the coach's role is vital. But how do we acquire these skills if we are to be the tutor?

1. Change our attitude. Understand clearly the difference between lecturing and coaching.

2. Understand the dimensions of the coaching role in PBL. Reflect on the different issues outlined at the beginning of this Chapter and the types of processing skills needed.

3. Accept that a good coach need not be a star player. How many basketball coaches were star players? What we want are excellent coaches. Some say to me, "But I am not that sure I am good at problem solving, or leading groups or solving interpersonal conflicts." You are not asked to solve problems, lead groups or resolve conflicts. You are asked to coach others in how to do that.

On the other hand, some potential tutors are excellent problem solvers, excellent resolvers of conflict and superb group leaders. But they often turn out to be ineffective tutors because they do not know how to coach or facilitate the process with the group.

4. Devote time to learning how to be a coach. Become skilled at bringing out the very best from your group.

Workshops designed to help tutors become good coaches can just as easily be run for students to develop their coaching/facilitation skills. The coaching skills are the processing skills (chairperson, conflict resolution, change management, problem solving, giving and receiving feedback).

Being an instructor with tutorless groups

If, because of class size, you function with tutorless groups, then your task is to create an environment to ensure that facilitation occurs by other means. You need to make the implicit explicit. If the tutor, as a member of the group, is trained to help the group resolve conflict; then in a tutorless group, the group members should receive this training. If the tutor is expected to probe the critical thinking of the group, then the group members need to be empowered to do this.

The overall role of the instructor is:

- To learn how tutored groups function, learn their challenges and make those challenges (and how to handle them) explicit.

- To provide training to the students about how to handle each issue; (instead of training the tutor, we train the students; maybe we train both.)

- To monitor, assess and provide feedback to the students about their ability. Just because the instructor is not a listening member within each group does not mean the instructor forsakes the role of monitor and assessor. All it means is that other avenues must be developed to achieve these goals. The instructor must hold the groups accountable for the activities we empower the student groups to do.

Summary

The facilitator/coach role must be present in any effective PBL group. The role is to bring out the very best from the group members. Research cited at the beginning of this Chapter outlines what particular facilitation skills the coach must supply. Wilkerson's research confirms the critical roles and skills needed.

For tutored groups, the faculty tutor usually supplies most of these skills. This requires an attitude shift from "lecturer" to "coach". Although many may intuitively possess these skills, tutor training helps to develop the coaching expertise.

For tutorless groups, the students receive the training in the process skills so as to bring out the very best in their groups. The tutor creates the learning environment for this to happen. The tutor monitors progress.

References

Barrows, H.S. and R.M. Tamblyn (1980) *Problem-based Learning: an approach to medical education.* Springer Publishing, New York, NY.

Coles, Colin (1991) *Beyond PBL* in *The Challenge of Problem-based Learning.* D. Boud and G. Feletti, eds., Kogan Page, London.

Covey, S. (1989) "The 7 Habits of Highly Effective People," Simon and Schuster, New York.

Dolmans, D.H.J.M. et al. (1993) "Problem Effectiveness in a Course Using Problem-based Learning," Academic Medicine, 68, 207-213.

Kimbell, R., K Stables, T. Wheeler, A, Wosniak and V. Kelly (1991) "The Assessment of Performance in Design and Technology," National Examination and Assessment Council, Newcombe House, London.

Schmidt, H.G. (1983) "Problem-based Learning: rationale and description", Medical Education, 17, 11-16.

Schoenfeld, A.H. (1984) "Episodes and Executive Decisions in Mathematical Problem Solving," in "Acquisition of Mathematics Concepts and Processes," R. Lesh and M. Landau, eds., Academic Press, New York.

Schon, D. (1987) "Educating the Reflective Practitioner: toward a new design for teaching and learning in the professions," Jossey-Bass, San Francisco.

Sparks, R. (1975) Washington University, St. Louis, personal communication.

Wilkerson, LuAnn (1994) "Identification of skills for the problem-based tutor: student and faculty perspectives," seminar, McMaster University, Hamilton, ON.

Woods, D.R. PS News 36 (1985) Newsletter published biannually by the Department of Chemical Engineering, McMaster University, Hamilton, ON., L8S 4L7.

Woods, D.R., "PS Corner", Journal of College Science Teaching, 13, May, 469-472 (1984)

Questioning Toolkit

Jamie McKenzie

What types of questions will equip our students with the ability to make sense of their complex worlds?

No one list could possibly identify every type required, in part because a changing world may demand new types of questions to fit new circumstances.

The list offered within this chapter is meant to be a beginning, not a final package. Each school should adopt a model of questioning that matches the age and readiness of its students, keeping in mind that even four year olds can (and often must) wrestle with incredibly demanding questions and issues if they are presented in terms and words that match their age.

Essential Questions	Subsidiary Questions	Hypothetical Questions	Telling Questions	Planning Questions
Organising Questions	Probing Questions	Sorting & Sifting Questions	Clarification Questions	Strategic Questions
Elaborating Questions	Unanswerable Questions	Inventive Questions	Provocative Questions	Irrelevant Questions
Divergent Questions	Irreverent Questions	As well as other types you find useful in the search for meaning.		

> **Different types of questions accomplish different tasks**
> **and help us to build up our answers in different ways.**

We must show our students the features of each type of question so they know which combination to employ with the essential question at hand. We don't want them reaching into their toolkit blindly, grasping the first question that comes to mind. No sense grabbing a screwdriver when a wrench is needed. No use seizing the hammer when a saw is required. We want them to reach for the question that matches the job.

Essential Questions

> **These are questions that touch our hearts and souls.**

They are central to our lives. They help to define what it means to be human. Most important thought during our lives will center on such Essential Questions.

- What does it mean to be a good friend?

- What kind of friend shall I be?

- Who will I include in my circle of friends?

- How shall I treat my friends?

- How do I cope with the loss of a friend?

- What can I learn about friends and friendships from the novels we read in school?

- How can I be a better friend?

When we draw a cluster diagram of the Questioning Toolkit, Essential Questions stand at the center of all the other types of questions. All the other questions and questioning skills serve the purpose of "casting light upon" or illuminating Essential Questions.

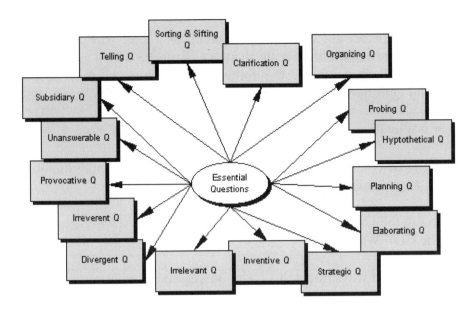

Most Essential Questions are interdisciplinary in nature. They cut across the lines created by schools and scholars to mark the terrain of departments and disciplines.

> **Essential Questions probe the deepest issues confronting us: complex and baffling matters that elude simple answers.**

Life - Death - Marriage - Identity - Purpose - Betrayal - Honor- Integrity - Courage - Temptation - Faith - Leadership - Addiction - Invention - Inspiration.

The greatest novels, the greatest plays, the greatest songs and the greatest paintings all explore Essential Questions in some manner. Essential Questions are at the heart of the search for Truth. Many of us believe that schools should devote more time to Essential Questions and less time to Trivial Pursuit. One major reform effort, the Coalition of Essential Schools, has made Essential Questions a keystone of its learning strategy.

Essential Questions offer the organizing focus for a unit.

If the U.S. History class will spend a month on a topic such as the Civil War, students explore the events and the experience with a mind toward casting light upon one of the following questions, or they develop Essential Questions of their own.

- Why do we have to fight wars?

- How could political issues or ideas ever become more important than family loyalties?

Some say the United States remains wounded by the slavery experience and the Civil War.

- In what ways might this claim be true and in what ways untrue?

- What evidence might substantiate your case?

Military officers often complain that political interference and popular pressures on the home front impede the effective conduct of modern war.

- To what extent did this also prove true during the Civil War?

- How can countries avoid the kind of bloodshed and devastation we experienced during the Civil War?

- Who showed greater bravery and courage, the front line soldiers and the nurses who tended to the wounded and dying or the leaders of the war effort?

- How much diversity can any nation tolerate?

- Should there be a law against war profiteering?

Subsidiary questions

These are questions that combine to help us build answers to our Essential Questions.

Big questions spawn families of smaller questions that lead to insight. The more skillful we and our students become at formulating and then categorizing subsidiary questions, the more success we will have constructing new knowledge.

All of the question categories listed and explained below are types of subsidiary questions. We have several strategies from which to choose when developing a comprehensive list of subsidiary questions for our project:

- We can brainstorm and list every question that comes to mind, utilizing a huge sheet of paper or a word processing program or a graphical organizing program such as Inspiration (http://www.inspiration.com), putting down the questions as they "come to mind." Later we can move these around until they end up along side of related questions. This movement is one advantage of software. This approach has the benefit of spontaneity.

- We can take a list of question categories like the one outlined in this article and generate questions for each category. This approach helps provoke thought and questions in categories that we might not otherwise consider.

In the (condensed) illustration that follows, a team is pondering the following Essential Question: What is the best way for our school to involve students in the use of e-mail? They begin by listing every question they can think up.

They have one member type the list into the outlining part of the software package, *Inspiration*. They could use a word processor instead, but *Inspiration* will automatically convert their outline into a variety of diagrams and will allow them to move questions around later.

What is the best way to involve students in the use of e-mail?

- Worst that can happen?

- Potential benefits?

- Obstacles that must be overcome?

- Available resources? Sufficient resources? Additional resources?

- Good models?

- How to prepare students? How to prepare parents?

- Relationship to discipline code?

- Timing?

- Who does what?

- Assessing progress.

This outline, using *Inspiration*, is transformed in seconds by a simple mouse click into a cluster diagram.

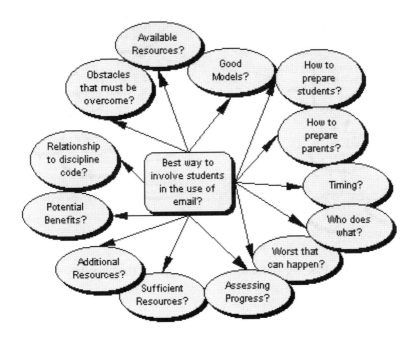

The lack of order and logic should be immediately visible. This diagram needs to be redrawn.

No problem. Point. Click. Drag!

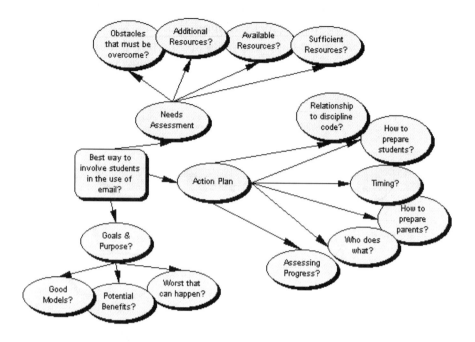

In just 4-5 minutes, we have a cluster diagram that groups questions.

Hypothetical Questions

These are questions designed to explore possibilities and test relationships. They usually project a theory or an option out into the future, wondering what might happen if ...

Suppose the earth had no moon. What if the South had won the Civil War?

Hypothetical Questions are especially helpful when trying to decide between a number of choices or when trying to solve a problem.

When we began to generate questions that would help us decide whether or not to offer e-mail accounts to our students, we asked ... What's the worst that might happen? What are the potential benefits? Hypothetical Questions are especially useful when we want to see if our hunches, our suppositions and our hypotheses have any merit.

Telling Questions

Telling Questions lead us right to the target.

They are built with such precision that they provide sorting and sifting during the gathering or discovery process. They focus the investigation so that we gather only the very specific evidence and information we require, only those facts that cast light upon or illuminate the main question at hand.

In schools that give students e-mail accounts, what is the rate of suspension for abusing the privilege? In schools that give students e-mail accounts, what percentage of students lose their privilege during each of the first ten months? Second ten months?

The better the list of telling questions generated by the researcher, the more efficient and pointed the subsequent searching and gathering process. A search strategy may be profoundly shifted by the development of telling questions.

As you can see below - students trying to rank the relative safety of ten cities in the Heartland will have greater success with their search if they translate their general question about crime: (Which city is safest?) into a Telling Question: (What is the violent crime rate for cities in New England as reported by the Federal Bureau of Justice and how has it changed over the past ten years?).

This would tend to be true whether they were searching on the free Internet or using an electronic encyclopedia or a pay-for-service collection of new articles.

> **The addition of precise elements to a search can radically reduce wasteful wandering.**

Search for General Question:
"crime" AND "cities" AND "Midwest"

Search for Telling Question:
"Bureau of Justice" AND "statistics" AND "homicides"

Planning Questions

> *Planning Questions lift us above the action of the moment and require that we think about how we will structure our search, where we will look and what resources we might use such as time and information.*

If we were sailing West on a square-masted ship, we would pass off the wheel and the lines to teammates in order to climb to the crow's nest - a lofty perch from which we could look over the horizon.

Too many researchers, be they student or adult, make the mistake of burying their noses in their studies and their sources. They have trouble seeing the forest, so close do they stand to the pine needles. They are easily lost in a thicket of possibilities.

The effective researcher develops a plan of action in response to Planning Questions like these:

Sources:
- Who has done the best work on this subject?

- Which group may have gathered the best information?

- Which medium (Internet, CD-ROM, electronic periodical collection, scholarly book, etc.) is likely to provide the most reliable and relevant information with optimal efficiency?

- Which search tool or index will speed the discovery process?

Sequence:
- What are all of the tasks that need completing in order to generate a credible product that offers fresh thought backed by solid evidence and sound thinking?

- What is the best way to organize these tasks over time? How much time is available? Which tasks come first, and then?

- Which tasks depend upon others or cannot be completed until others are finished?

Pacing:
- How much time is available for this project?

- How long does it take to complete each of the tasks required?

- How much time can be applied to each task?

- Do some tasks require more care and attention than others?

- Can some tasks be rushed?

- Is it possible to complete the project in the time available?

- How should the plan be changed to match the time resources?

Organizing Questions

> **Organizing Questions make it possible to structure our findings into categories that will allow us to construct meaning.**

Without these structures we suffer from hodge-podge and mish-mash - information collections akin to trash heaps and landfills, large in mass, lacking in meaning. The less structure we create in the beginning, the harder it becomes later to find patterns and relationships in the fragments or the collection of bits and pieces.

If we are trying to compare and contrast three cities (or three products or three bills or three artists) we might use our criteria and our telling questions as the basis for the fields and the entries in our database. Or we may develop a word processing file around these criteria and questions that becomes the collecting mechanism for our findings.

Cities Database: Source/ Subject/ Keywords/ Abstract

Each time we come upon valuable findings, we extract the relevant data and place them where they belong. If we find facts about the violent crime rate in Portland, for example, we enter them along with their source as a record in the database that might look something like this:

Cities Database:

Source: Money Online: Best Places: Money ranks the 300 biggest places - URL: http://www.pathfinder.com/

Subject words: Portland Crime

Keywords: violent crime rate

Abstract: 270.5 crimes per 100,000 people vs. 716 crimes National average.

Our challenge is teaching students to paraphrase, condense and then place their findings thoughtfully, rather than cutting and pasting huge blocks of text that have been unread, undigested and undistilled.

Probing Questions

**Probing Questions take us below the surface
to the heart of the matter.**

They operate somewhat like the archeologist's tools - the brushes that clear away the surface dust and the knives that cut through the accumulated grime and debris to reveal the outlines and ridges of some treasure.   Another appropriate metaphor might be "exploratory surgery".

The good doctor spends little time on the surface, knowing full well that the vital organs reside at a deeper level. We never stop investigating. We are never satisfied that we know enough to get by.

Every question we answer leads on to another question. This has become the greatest survival trick of our species.
(Desmond Morris)

**The search for insight involves
some of the same exploratory elements.**

We look for the same kind of "convergence" that guides oil prospecting. The geologist knows that the odds of finding oil are greatly increased when three or four elements are all present in the same location.

When it comes to information seeking, the convergence is established by creating a logical intersection of search words and key concepts, the combination of which is most likely to identify relevant sites and articles.

> **Probing Questions allow us to push search strategies well beyond the broad topical search to something far more pointed and powerful.**

And when we first encounter an information "site," we rarely find the treasures lying out in the open within easy reach. We may need to "feel for the vein" much as the lab technician tests before drawing blood. This "feeling" is part logic, part prior knowledge, part intuition and part trial-and-error.

Logic: We check to see if there is any structure to the way the information is organized and displayed, if there are any signposts or clues pointing to where the best information resides. We assume the author had some plan or design to guide placement of information and we try to identify its outlines.

Prior Knowledge: We apply what we have seen and known in the past to guide our search. We consider information about the topic and prior experience with information sites. This prior knowledge helps us to avoid dead ends and blind alleys. It helps us to make wise choices when browsing through lists of "hits."

> **Prior knowledge also makes it easier to interpret new findings, to place them into a context and distinguish between "fool's gold" and the real thing.**

Intuition: We explore our hunches, follow our instincts, look for patterns and connections, and make those leaps our minds can manage. Especially when we are hoping to create new knowledge and carve out new insights, this non-rational, nonlogical form of information harvesting is critically important.

Trial-and-error: Sometimes, nothing works better than plain old experimentation. Push here. Tug there. Try this out! We find a site with so much information and so little structure that we have little choice but to plunge in and see what we can find.

Sorting & Sifting Questions

Sorting & Sifting Questions enable us to manage Infoglut and Info-Garbage - the hundreds of hits and pages and files that often rise to the surface when we conduct a search - culling and keeping only the information that is pertinent and useful.

> *Relevancy is the primary criterion employed to determine which pieces of information are saved and which are tossed overboard.*

We create a "net" of questions that allows all but the most important information to slide away. We then place the good information with the questions it illuminates.

- Which parts of this data are worth keeping?

- Will this information shed light on any of my questions?"

- Is this information reliable?

- How much of this information do I need to place in my database?

- How can I summarize the best information and ideas?

- Are there any especially good quotations to paste in the abstract field?

Clarification Questions

Clarification Questions convert fog and smog into meaning.

A collection of facts and opinions does not always make sense by itself. Hits do not equal TRUTH. A mountain of information may do more to block understanding than promote it.

- Defining words and concepts is central to this clarification process.

- What do they mean by "violent crime rate?" Do they use the same definition and standards as the FBI?

- What do they mean by "declining rate of increase?"

- How did they gather their data? Was it a reliable and valid process? Do they show the data and evidence they claim to have in support of their conclusions? Was it substantial enough to justify their conclusions?

- Did they gather evidence and data?

Examining the coherence and logic of an argument, an article, an essay, an editorial or a presentation is fundamental.

- How did they develop the case they are presenting?

- What is the sequence of ideas and how do they relate one to another?

- Do the ideas logically follow one from the other?

Determining the underlying assumptions is vital.

- How did they get to this point?

- Are there any questionable assumptions below the surface or at the foundation of the argument?

Clever people seem not to feel the natural pleasure of bewilderment, and are always answering questions when the chief relish of a life is to go on asking them.   (Frank Moore Colby)

Strategic Questions

Strategic Questions focus on ways to make meaning.

The researcher must switch from tool to tool and strategy to strategy while passing through unfamiliar territory. Closely associated with the planning questions formulated early on in this process, Strategic Questions arise during the actual hunting, gathering, inferring, synthesising and ongoing questioning process.

- What do I do next?

- How can I best approach this next step? this next challenge? this next frustration?

- What thinking tool is most apt to help me here?

- What have I done when I've been here before? What worked or didn't work? What have others tried before me?

- What type of question would help me most with this task?

- How do I need to change my research plan?

Elaborating Questions

Elaborating Questions extend and stretch the import of what we are finding.

They take the explicit and see where it might lead. They also help us to seek below the surface to implicit (unstated) meanings:

- What does this mean?

- What might it mean if certain conditions and circumstances changed?

- How could I take this farther? What is the logical next step? What is missing? What needs to be filled in?

- Reading between the lines, what does this REALLY mean?

- What are the implied or suggested meanings?

Unanswerable Questions

Unanswerable Questions are the ultimate challenge.

They serve like boundary stones, helping us to know when we have pushed insight to its outer limits. When exploring Essential Questions (most of which are unanswerable in the ultimate sense), we may have to settle for "casting light" upon them.

When wrestling with these Unanswerable Questions, we may never find Truth, but we may illuminate - extend the level of understanding and reduce the intensity of the darkness.

The real questions are the ones that obtrude upon your consciousness whether you like it or not, the ones that make your mind start vibrating like a jackhammer, the ones that you "come to terms with" only to discover that they are still there.

The real questions refuse to be placated. They barge into your life at the times when it seems most important for them to stay away. They are the questions asked most frequently and answered most inadequately, the ones that reveal their true natures slowly, reluctantly, most often against your will. (Ingrid Bengis)

- How will I be remembered?

- How much can anyone resist Fate's will?

- What is the Good Life?

- What is friendship?

- How would life be different if . . .

Students wrestling with Essential Questions must be prepared for the strong likelihood that their questions may be Unanswerable. They must be taught that this reality is perfectly acceptable and is no signal to stop searching and thinking.

Inventive Questions

Inventive Questions turn our findings inside out and upside down.

They distort, modify, adjust, rearrange, alter, twist and turn the bits and pieces we have picked up along the way until we can shout "Aha!" and proclaim the discovery of something brand new.

- How do I make sense of these bits and bytes and pieces?

- What does all this information really mean?

- How can I rearrange what I have gathered so that some picture or new insight emerges?

- What needs to be eliminated or reversed or modified in order to make better sense of my findings?

- What is still missing?

- Can any information be regrouped or combined in ways that help meaning to emerge?

- Can I display this information or data in a way that will cast more light on my essential question?

Provocative Questions

> **Provocative Questions are meant to push, to challenge and to throw conventional wisdom off balance. They give free rein to doubt, disbelief and skepticism.**

The best servants of the people, like the best valets, must whisper unpleasant truths in the master's ear. It is the court fool, not the foolish courtier, whom the king can least afford to lose.

(Walter Lippmann)

Ancient empires and kingdoms in China often employed a court jester or fool whose job it was to challenge and make fun of policies and ideas and key players surrounding the king or queen.

The fool could often get away with a level of questioning that would never have been permitted a "legitimate" member of the council. On the other hand, the fool might also lose his head if the king or queen took offense. A dangerous occupation!

Closely associated with Divergent Questions and Irreverent Questions, Provocative Questions help provide the basis for satire, parody, and expose whether it be *Gulliver's Travels, Alice in Wonderland,* or *Dilbert.*

These plays and stories poke fun at politicians and leaders in ways that help protect us from excessive deference or what is called "spin" today.

In the case of student research, we have probably devoted too little attention to irony, satire and parody as an important element in "open systems," a term that describes responsive (and healthy) political systems as well as organizations of various kinds such as schools and corporations.

> *When inspired by a desire to understand the Truth, Provocative Questions play a positive role in debunking propaganda, mythologies, hype, bandwagons and the Big Lie.*

They help us to remove the "bunk" or "claptrap" and determine if there is any substance worth considering. In a time of what Toffler calls "info-tactics" such questions become an essential tool for any citizen in a democratic society.

In an age of info-glut and info-garbage, we must equip students with questions that enable them to separate out meaning from all the competing variants of BLATHER (quoted here from Roget's Thesaurus) . . .

> *empty talk, idle speeches, sweet nothings, endearments, wind, gas, hot air, vaporing, verbiage, DIFFUSENESS rant, ranting and raving, bombast, fustian, rodomontade, BOASTING, blether, blather, blah-blah-blah, flimflam, guff, hogwash, eyewash, claptrap, poppycock, FABLE humbug*

- Where's the beef? content? substance? logic? evidence?

- What is the source? Is the source reliable?

- What's the point? Is there a point?

- Cutting past the noise and the rhetoric, is there any insight, knowledge or worthwhile information here?

Irrelevant Questions

Irrelevant Questions take us far afield, distract us and threaten to divert us from the task at hand.

And that is their beauty!

Truth almost never appears where we might look logically. The creation of new knowledge almost always requires some wandering off course. The more we cling to coastline, the less apt we are to find the New World. As Melville so dramatically pointed out in *Moby Dick*, the search for Truth requires the courage to venture out and away from the familiar and the known.

But as in landlessness alone resides the highest truth, shoreless, indefinite as God — so, better is it to perish in that howling infinite, than be ingloriously dashed upon the lee, even if that were safety! (Melville)

Divergent Questions

> **Divergent Questions use existing knowledge as a base from which to kick off like a swimmer making a turn.**

They move more logically from the core of conventional knowledge and experience than irrelevant questions. They are more carefully planned to explore territory that is adjacent to that which is known or understood.

Trying to find a way to restore water quality in a lake or stream? If we limit our search to successful attempts, we may miss out on the chance to avoid other people's mistakes. Sometimes we learn more by studying the opposite of our main target.

In the same sense, we may want to check out efforts to restore air quality and other tangentially related efforts. We may even explore efforts to reintroduce endangered species to various habitats. New ideas are rarely sitting waiting for us in obvious places. The ability to freely associate related topics and questions greatly increases the odds that researchers will make important discoveries.

Irreverent Questions

Irreverent Questions explore territory that is "off-limits" or taboo.

They challenge far more than conventional wisdom. They hold no respect for authority or institutions or myths. They leap over, under or through walls and rules and regulations.

Socrates found himself in considerable trouble for showing the youth of Athens how to ask Irreverent Questions, and we need to remember that such questions are not universally appreciated. In fact, some folks find such questioning disrespectful and impolite. They question the value of Irreverent Questions.

It is the human condition to question one god after another, one appearance after another, or better, one apparition after another, always pursuing the truth of the imagination, which is not the same as the truth of appearance.

Alain [Émile-Auguste Chartier]

Corporations like IBM have learned that today's heretic - the one with the courage, the tenacity and the brash conviction to question the way things are "spozed to be" - often turns out to be a prophet of sorts. *The Emperor's New Clothes* is the classic story showing what happens when Irreverent Questions are discouraged and obedience, subservience and compliance are prized. The emperor parades naked. The corporation clings blindly to old beliefs.

References

ASLA and AECT. (1998). *Information Power: Building Partnerships for Learning,* Chicago, American Library Association.

Barron, Dan, *Information Literacy: Dan's Generic Model,* University of South Carolina.

Bloom, B. (1954). *Taxonomy of Educational Objectives. Handbook I: Cognitive Domain,* New York, Longmans, Green & Co.

Brooks, M. and Brooks, J. (1993). *In search of Understanding: the Case for constructivist Classrooms,* Alexandria, VA:ASCD.

Bruner, Jerome (1990). *Acts of Meaning,* Cambridge: Harvard University Press.

Culham, Ruth and Spandel, Vicki. *The Six Traits Writing Model.* Materials available from the NWREL at *http://nwrel.org/eval/writing/products.html*

Dewey, John (1916) *Democracy and education.* Reprint edition, Vol 009, October 1985, Southern Illinois Press.

Eberle, Bob (1997). *SCAMPER,* Prufrock Press

Eisenberg, M and Berkowitz, R., (1990). *Information Problem-Solving: The Big Six Skills Approach to Library and Information Skills Instruction,* Abblex Publishing: Norwood, NJ.

Fenton, Edwin. *Teaching the New Social Studies in Secondary Schools: an Inductive Approach.*

Goodlad, J. (1984). *A Place Called School,* Highstown, NJ: McGraw-Hill.

Henley, S. and Thompson, H. (2000). *Fostering Information Literacy: Connecting National Standards, Goals 2000 and the SCANS Report,* Libraries Unlimited.

Hyman, r. (1980). Fielding Student Questions. *Theory into Practice,* 1: 38-44.

Infozone from the Assiniboine South School Division of Winnipeg, Canada. *http://www.mbnet.mb.ca/~mstimson/*

Keen & Zimmerman. (1997). *Mosaic of Thought: Teaching Comprehension in a Reader's Workshop.*

Langford, Linda. Information Literacy: A Clarification. In *School Libraries Worldwide,* 4(1).

Learning for the Future: Developing Information Services in Australian Schools. (1993). Curriculum Corp.

Loertscher, David. *The Organized Investigator.* (Circular Model). California Technology Assistance Project.
At *http://ctap.fcoe.k12.ca.us/ctap/Info.Lit/infolit.html*

Loertscher, David. (2000) *Taxonomies of the School Library Media Program,* San Jose: Hi Willow research & Publishing.

McKenzie, Jamie. (1999). *How Teachers Learn Technology Best,* Bellingham, WA: FNO Press.

McKenzie, Jamieson. (1993). *Power Learning,* Newbury Park, California: Corwin Press.

NCREL (North Central Regional Educational Lab). (1995). *Plugging In.*

Pappas, Marjorie and Tepe, Ann. Pathways to Knowledge, Follett's Information Skills Model. At *http://www.pathwaysmodel.com/*

Postman, Neil and Weingartner, Charles. (1969). *Teaching as a Subversive Activity,* New York: Delacorte Press.

Problems of Readiness and Preparation, (1999). The September 1999 Report of Market Data Retrieval.

Shenk, David. (1997). *Data Smog,* New York: Harper Edge.

Sizer, Theodore. (1984). *Horace's Compromise,* Boston: Houghton Mifflin Co.

Taba, Hilda. (1988). A Conceptual Framework for Curriculum Design, *Curriculum: An Introduction to the Field*, ed. James R. Gress, Berkeley, CA: McCutchan Publishing Corporation, 276-304.

Toffler, A. (1990). *Power Shift,* New York: Bantam Books.

Wyatt, Edward. (1999). Encyclopedia Green: The High Road at a High Cost, *New York Times,* October 24, 1999.

Assessing learning: Points for consideration

James Henri

Introduction

In an earlier paper (Henri: 1999) I argued that:

> *The process of assessment provides the opportunity to verify that learning has occurred. Assessment of learning might occur at the conclusion of a teaching/learning program. It may occur during the learning process and it may occur prior to the learning task. A combination of the three moments will provide the richest and most accurate picture of the impact of the program upon the learner and will provide the best evidence of the impact of the teaching process.*

In one sense this might suggest that assessment can become overwhelming, and it can. This was not my intention, however, because I believe that over-assessment is a disease. Teachers must find ways to economise on assessment. At the same time learning needs to be 'tested' and this means that assessment is a vital and integral part of learning and teaching.

Setting the scene: A case study

You have been teaching for fifteen years and have had a variety of appointments. Your current appointment is at a large urban school located in a recently completed estate. You were appointed three years ago and hold the position of curriculum coordinator.

30% of the student population consists of students whose parents were born in the area. The other 70% represent 'new arrivals' from 23 countries. English is the second, third or fourth language for most of these students.

Your colleague, Sue, is reviewing a unit of study on pollution. The last time Sue taught this unit she included a number of visits to a nearby industrial area. Some of the students have family members employed in the estate. These visits were carefully planned and included the opportunity to visit people in their workplaces. The visits brought the study of pollution out of the theoretical confines of the classroom and placed it into an authentic setting. Students were required to measure pollution levels and to analyse their short-term and longer-term effects on the residents and workers in the area.

Assessment in the unit was very varied and included: maintaining a journal of questions and reflections, recording observations of air, sound, and water pollution, and included consideration of the treatment of industrial waste.

Students were given training in interviewing techniques and used these skills to interview a number of people. Interviews, which were taped, were conducted in pairs with the silent partner writing reflections of the process.

Sue had given much thought to the assessment of the unit. She had gained the principal's support to feature this unit in the bi-annual Open Day that had the theme 'reclaiming our world'. The intention was to feature innovative ideas and to provide public recognition of the students' achievements.

The students had a reasonably free hand to present their findings in a way that best achieved their purpose. Presentations included: posters, a special edition of 'the world around us' a desktop published newspaper, oral presentations and written reports, and a debate with the theme 'pollution is a necessary bi-product of economic growth'.

The debate was conducted as part of an inter-school competition.

While Sue had provided considerable latitude to the class in defining the focus of their learning she feels that she would like to give even greater ownership to the students by involving them in the assessment of the work. However, she has no experience in this area. Sue regards you as a mentor and has called on you for advice about her approach to assessment and the legitimacy of what she is doing. She is reasonably happy with the unit but feels she can do better and wants to offer more ownership to her students.

As you ponder the specifics that Sue has laid out you are already going back to basics. You mull over the following points:

- *Taking into account the freedom that your colleague has given, and the additional responsibility she wants to offer to the students in defining their own assessment, how can she be confident that her students know what is expected of them?*

- *Did the previous forms of assessment provide reliable evidence about the achievement of expected learning outcomes, both process and product?*

- *What options are available that would facilitate student ownership of the assessment without jeopardising authenticity?*

It is widely accepted that Sue is a leading educator in your school and you are honoured that she regards you as a mentor. While some of your colleagues lack imagination with respect to methods of instruction and rewarding learning, this colleague is ready to experiment and take risks if she believes that this will result in better learning outcomes. There is no 'duck feeding' or 'spoon feeding' in your colleague's classes.

> **At the heart of her personal philosophy is a deep desire to facilitate student learning and the taking on of ownership for that learning by the student.**

This is in stark contrast to some other practice at school.

> **Some teachers are not even aware that there is a difference between measuring what a student knows at the completion of a Unit of Work and what a student has learned during that Unit.**

Some colleagues have not ventured beyond summative assessment because other in-depth methods are too messy or difficult. These colleagues seem unaware that a prerequisite to effective teaching is an ability and willingness to know a student well enough to be able to judge what has been learned.

This process entails at least two considerations: knowing what the student knew at the beginning of the learning task, and being able to gauge how that student's understanding has developed through the learning.

> **Good teachers are facilitators of learning who want to use their assessments to provide insights into the skill and knowledge of their students.**

Ingredients of quality assessment

Stiggins (2001) identifies five key ingredients of, or ways of judging, quality assessment. These are posed in the form of questions: what, why, how, how much, and how accurate is the assessment.

While it might seem obvious that a teacher should commence planning for learning with a discussion about learning targets the reality is that often this is not what is considered first. Many teachers actually begin considerations with discussion about activities or with what students like to do.

Any chance that a teacher has of assessing learning rests, at a very fundamental level, on being clear about what it is that is expected of the learner.

> *In its simplest form the question is 'what do I want the student to learn?' Only when this fundamental question is placed on the table is it appropriate to think about 'what should be assessed?'*

A task, or unit of work, must be clear enough and specific enough to define what to teach and to let students know what they need to learn. As Stripling (1999: 44) notes this can entail more than thinking about content objectives.

She asks:

...what would they need to know and be able to do to complete [the learning] successfully? Who is teaching your students to find and evaluate information, to interpret primary source documents and photographs, to access such documents electronically, to use researched evidence in a new product? Do you think your students have these skills? How will you find if they do and if they can apply those skills to new situations?

A challenge for the teacher is to frame the unit in terms that are broad enough to allow for some flexibility and individualism, yet still specific enough to guide the learner in the right direction. Once the unit is well defined the teacher needs to consider 'what would count as evidence that the unit has been learned'?

The second ingredient that needs to be considered is the purpose for assessing the learning.

> **A teacher must make choices and one of those is to consider why learning in this unit needs assessing at all.**

And if it is to be assessed how will the knowledge gained from that assessment be used?' Also to be considered is the amount of control by the learners over their assessment.

The third ingredient considers the match between expected learning outcomes and the methods of assessment.

> **Which methods of assessment are most appropriate for each kind of outcome?**

How does assessment do justice to the efficiency of learning (including consideration of learning style and intelligence) as well as to the outcome of the learning? The following assessment genres (following Stiggins, 1997) might be considered:

• **Formal writing:** This genre, which is evidenced by essays and reports, generally involves using writing as the tool for expressing knowledge of content, conceptual understanding, and thinking. This genre is often used as a means to gauge higher order thinking skills, especially synthesis. But if the assessment is poorly constructed it will probably result in copy and paste.

• **Performance:** This genre is associated with 'learning by doing'. Both product and process can be examined by performance and often it is the only authentic way to judge learning. How else do you judge learning to swim? Performance can be showcased in posters, graphs, video, web pages, and power-point presentations. Debates, drama, laboratory experiments, mime, orals, plays, and sport, provide the means for demonstrating process learning.

- **Selected response:** The selected response genre includes multiple-choice tests, true or false quizzes, and short answer formats. This genre is useful as a device for checking knowledge, but weak as a measure of higher order thinking skills.

- **Dialogue:** This genre offers personal insight through engagement with the learner. Strategies used within this genre might include discussing, questioning, group conferencing, interviewing and listening. A learner who is better at writing than at speaking, or who needs considerable 'think-time', is disadvantaged by this genre.

- **Self-reflection:** This genre places responsibility onto the learner to use personal and private tools to monitor learning and to raise questions. In its purest form self-reflection becomes self-assessment. Self-reflection tools include: think-aloud protocols, diaries and journals, thinking logs and scaffolding tools such as self generated rubrics.

- **Drafts:** This genre cuts across the preceding genres in the sense that any of those tools can be associated with drafting. The focus of this genre is the point. While the other genres tend to be used to measure learning outcomes, drafting is employed to check learning progress. It facilitates risk-taking and removes the threat of a once off assessment. Drafting does not ignore the products of learning but it places the spotlight on the processes that the learner uses to learn and provides opportunity for revision and review. Examples of drafting might include: an essay outline, notes, critiquing, data charts, ideas presented on audio cassette, as well as first drafts of products such as sketches.

Stripling (1999: 48-49) argues strongly for the use of drafting as a way of dealing with the temptation to copy. She states:

Plagiarism in the electronic age is easy and is not easily detected. Students should be taught the principles of intellectual freedom and copyright, and should be held to those standards. Teachers ... can try to safeguard by asking students for all drafts of a work with written or visual elements by spot-checking sources.

A much more effective technique is to construct assignments so they cannot be copied (who could find a recipe, for Abraham Lincoln's life, on the Internet?).

Probably the most effective safeguard is to arrange exhibitions and presentations of research projects that students defend through questioning and dialogue.

Callison (1994a: 54-55) builds this idea by pointing to the complexity of assessment in the real world.

He argues that not only is the process complex but often it needs to be collaborative because a single assessor will not have the skill-set to cover the complexity of the learning.

He states:

New methods of evaluation should be explored because students may be judged on questioning techniques, search and location strategies, listening skills, organization skills, scripting and editing skills, and presentation methods. Just as a house is appraised and valued at several stages of construction, so too is the process by which students and teachers construct knowledge and intelligence from the information surrounding them. Foundation, framework, and finished product each have need for new appraisal instruments and new collaborative appraisers who have an inquiry method orientation.

> **Motivation for learning is the key to successful learning and assessment must not be allowed to hinder that motivation.**

Good assessment, and the feedback that it can provide, leads to improved instruction and opportunities for students to learn. To that end it is essential that a teacher vary the forms of assessment. This is necessary for reasons of fairness and is a sound way of combating boredom with assessment methods.

The fourth ingredient for quality assessment is to create a good balance between learning and assessment. One balance is between over and under assessing the learner. The teacher may be so interested in assessing learning that the learner's focus shifts from learning to assessment. The danger here is that the assessment becomes the learning, rather than a measure of that learning.

Under assessment occurs when the form of assessment does not provide the learner with accurate feedback on the learning. Often a single test or sample of work is unlikely to provide sufficient accuracy about what the learner knows and is able to do for any given learning target.

> **Sufficient sampling is needed to make sound inferences about learning.**

A further consideration is the balance between the quality of feedback to the learner and the timeliness of that feedback. Conscientious teachers strive to give fulsome feedback. The timing of this feedback is, however, crucial. It is crucial to the extent that the learner can respond to it. If all feedback occurs after the completion of the learning then it will only impact the learner to the extent that it is linked to future learning tasks. This is why drafting and process feedback is important because it can be used as a checkpoint that allows a change in direction, or in focus, or perhaps in attitude.

The 'intensity' of the feedback is important too. A quick response may have more impact than a more articulate and considered, but slower response.

> **The purpose of the learning, the assessment, and the feedback, must be carefully considered if the teacher is to get this difficult balancing act right.**

Ingredient five deals with the question of the accuracy of the assessment. Are the set of assessment tools actually measuring what the teacher wants to measure? How accurate are the assessments? Is there anything about the assessment that may result in an inaccurate understanding of the learning that has occurred?

The teacher and the learner need to know whether or not the teaching/learning process associated with any particular planned learning agenda provides a new experience. It is after all new experiences that provide the opportunity for new understanding, new meaning, and new knowledge.

> **Teachers must decide whether they want to measure what was learned as a result of the unit or whether they want to measure student knowledge and understanding independently of what transpired during the unit.**

The latter is simpler but it undermines the craft of teaching because it does not provide feedback about the effectiveness of the teaching to progress learning. The former is complex and it shifts the emphasis away from the quality of the outcome towards the quality of the learning. This shift is based upon the belief that assessment that concentrates on outcomes produces a culture of winners and losers.

> **Assessment that pays attention to, and rewards, the learning that occurs within a unit leads to a culture of continuous improvement and is likely to motivate a passion for life long learning.**

A mismatch occurs when the assessment is aimed to measure learning but actually measures knowledge. A common example is demonstrated by the teacher who assesses learning in spelling by issuing a spelling test and rewarding those who gain the highest scores. What is actually being measured is knowledge. An alternative approach to assessment would be to reward knowledge by issuing a pre-test. A post-test would then identify the improvement in spelling. Without some form of pre-test the student who scores 30% on the test but could not spell any of the chosen words prior to the unit will not gain the notice of the teacher. Those who score 100% will gain attention even though they may have known how to spell most of the words prior to the unit. (Of course the teacher needs to be smart enough to know when a student deliberately underscores on a pre-test!)

> *A mismatch occurs when the expected learning is not matched by the students information skill set.*

Stripling (1999) notes the research findings (Pitts 1994) that indicate

> *'that students are hampered in their learning of content if it is isolated from process skills lessons. Students who are expected to produce a videotape about a wastewater treatment plant, for example, cannot learn about wastewater effectively if they are distracted by their lack of videotaping skills.'*

Biases need to be reconsidered and so do ethical standards stemming from temptations to cloud or shade evidence through editing and lifting out of context. Process assessment should include examination of the merits of resources identified and used and considerations for seeking access to resources initially beyond reach. Callison (1996a: 54) asks 'did the student make the extra effort to obtain what was previously off limits?'

> **A further mismatch can occur when the level of reasoning required by the teacher is not clearly articulated or understood in the instructions or reflected in the result of the task itself.**

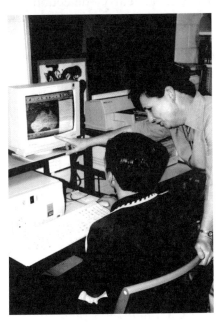

Understanding of thinking, whether in terms of a taxonomy, (Bloom: 1956) or in terms of style, (de Bono: 1987) or in terms of intelligences, (Gardiner: 1983), is crucial.

The teacher for example, may be looking for analysis but receives application. Or the teacher may want comprehension but gets knowledge. Every form of assessment can create bias and distortion, and sometimes this is difficult for a single teacher to detect.

A mismatch between the instructional expectations and assessment can occur for many reasons. When this does occur the assessment does not provide the feedback the teacher intended, nor does it provide what the learner needed. Some of these potential distortions are under the control of the teacher.

Consideration to the following factors will help to minimize unintentional bias:

- Are the students clear about what is important?
  (Diez and Moon: 1992)

- Do all the students have the requisite skill-set needed to complete the tasks? What measures will be taken to address any skill deficit?

- Are there checkpoints to enable early detection of problems?

- Do the checkpoints address the three learning domains: actions, thoughts, and feelings (Kuhlthau: 1993).

- Does what is being measured adequately represent the key elements of the unit?

- Is the 'prettiness' of the product or the accuracy of grammar and syntax overemphasized?

- Are all instructions written? Is the language clear and non-technical? If the instructions are lengthy, or if the response is required in written form, will that disadvantage 'new arrivals'?

- Does the assessment cater to each student's predominant learning style or intelligence? If not, is this justifiable? Is the 'context' of the assessment clear to all learners including 'new arrivals'?

- Has audience been considered? Is a single instructor equipped to undertake the assessment?

- Is the assessment flexible enough to allow for non-conventional learners?

- Is there sufficient evidence that the learner has undertaken the work? Is adequate attention being paid to copying and 'family help'?

The generation of assessment rubrics is one way to address some of the potential bias that is identified above. For the uninitiated teacher the development of a rubric can be formidable.

However, the Chicago Board of Education (2000) has developed a useful set of steps and links to enable the process.

The steps they identify are:
With your colleagues, make a preliminary decision on the dimensions of the performance or product to be assessed.

1. Look at some actual examples of student work to see if you have omitted any important dimensions.

2. Refine and consolidate your list of dimensions as needed. Write a definition of each of the dimensions.

3. Develop a continuum (scale) for describing the range of products/ performances on each of the dimensions.

4. Alternatively, instead of a set of rating scales, you may choose to develop a holistic scale or a checklist on which you will record the presence or absence of the attributes of a quality product/performance.

5. Evaluate your rubric using the criteria discussed in step 1.

6. Pilot test your rubric or checklist on actual samples of student work.

7. Revise the rubric and try it out again.

8. Share the rubric with your students and their parents.

Is good assessment, authentic assessment?

To what extent is assessment that meets the criteria of quality assessment actually authentic? Henri (1996: 110) argued that:

> *Authentic assessment is designed to provide a reliable measure of a student's understanding and may encompass a range of techniques including testing of key concepts, observations, ratings, interviews, questionnaires, and performances.*
>
> *Within this paradigm students become much more involved in the assessment process. They contribute to decisions about what is important and what part of their achievement should be measured.*

> **Because of its emphasis on real-life learning and reflection on that learning, authentic assessment changes content and teaching strategies.**

Teachers become more reflective about how their instructional practice is facilitating learning, and about how well their assessment instruments are measuring that learning and motivating students to want to learn. In the best situations teachers give up their role as a 'director of traffic' and become involved in the learning process. This blurring of the distinction between teaching and learning provides the teacher with a powerful window into the learning milieu.

To what extent will the criteria of quality assessment provide opportunities for 'life like' experience? In what way is the learning benchmarked? To what extent does the learner have control over that learning? How authentic is the assessment 'audience'?

Benchmarking assessment

You are troubled about some aspects of your colleague's assessment and make a note that you need to check the detail of the assessment to see how well the tasks are explained, especially given the large percentage of 'new arrivals' in the school. You ponder the issue of how Sue is able to compare and contrast students' achievement given the great variety of approaches to assessment. This raises the issue of the need for some form of benchmarking.

> **The standard approaches to benchmarking are to employ either a criterion-reference or a norm-reference.**

The former benchmarks a measurement of achievement of specific criteria or skills in terms of absolute levels of mastery. The focus is on performance of an individual as measured against a standard or criteria rather than against performance of others who take the same test. The criteria can accommodate both process and product elements. The latter is an objective test that is standardized on a group of individuals whose performance is evaluated in relation to the performance of others.

A norm-reference is justifiable in those circumstances that require winners and losers.

> **The use of a criterion-referenced benchmark provides the opportunity for a community of winners and is likely to facilitate the employment of group work and other forms of collegial problem solving.**

Stripling (1999) discusses the efficacy of standards-based teaching as a form of criterion-referenced benchmarking. In her discussion she refers to the need to benchmark information skills and refers to the AASL document *The Nine Information Literacy Standards for Student Learning* that can be adopted by individual schools.

Extensive work on developing information skill benchmarks has been undertaken in Canada. These include the development of a *Student Bill of Rights* (ATLC: 1995), an information studies curriculum (OSLA: 1998), and a comprehensive system wide approach to information literacy developed in Prince Edward Island (1998).

Lupton (1996), in arguing for the benchmarking of a school wide approach to integrating information skills into assessable work, identified the need for teachers to look to information specialists as collaborators in the process of assessment.

He suggested that:

> *As information literacy specialists, teacher librarians input to student learning will necessarily be related to advocacy for, and support of, the implementation of a model of the information process which is consistently developed across the curriculum and year levels.*

> *Part of this approach should also involve the inclusion of check points in assessment tasks to monitor mastery of the steps in the information process, a process [in which] skills continue to expand as the modes of information delivery expand.*

Recent research certainly indicates that teachers' expectations for their own learning, vis-à-vis information skills, do not generally match what they expect from their students. (McGregor 1994, O'Connell & Henri 1997).

> **It could be argued that teachers ought to be much more expert in their understanding of the information process through personal experience and this lack of expertise may be a roadblock to the introduction of authentic assessment.**

Stripling (1994: 90) proposed a further reason for the involvement of the teacher librarian in the assessment process. She argued that:

Because performance-based assessments should be evaluated by someone without a vested interest, the [teacher librarian] helps the students and classroom teachers by filling that role whenever possible. [Teacher librarians] also evaluate written student products, especially those based on research in the library.

Certainly the teacher librarian ought to be well placed to make judgements about studentsí questions, the sources pursued, and the evidence that was gathered to address the issues.

Callison (1994:128) reinforces this point:

In order for educators to establish meaningful information literacy exercises that challenge the student, assessment is best undertaken by means of a progressive portfolio of student's work. Both the teacher and the [teacher librarian] must think in terms of assignments that establish a broad range of sources the student will need to investigate and that are developed in recognition of the equally broad range of responses the student might produce.

Of major importance are the techniques of modelling information literacy skills developed by the teacher and the [teacher librarian] and the establishment of inquiry environments in which students work together in order to explore and share the challenges of information search and selection...

The time is ripe to go beyond the simple tests of the past in our explorations of what can be observed, what can be discussed, and what abilities can be enhanced.

The argument is that teacher librarians are personally acquainted with the messiness of the information process from their own teaching and learning. A similar argument could be mounted for the consideration of the involvement of other specialists as part of a collegial assessment team.

It may be appropriate to appoint a small committee of teachers as an assessment panel (or a sub-committee of the Curriculum Committee) with responsibility to consider drafts of assessment tools and to provide feedback on their quality. In this way assessment is much more school focused than teacher focused and provides the opportunity for quicker adoption of new ideas and of standards. It ensures that assessment is valued. Copies of units of study, including samples of student assessment, for reference by teachers and students, could be maintained on the Intranet or in the school library.

Does the learner own the process?

Your colleague, Sue, has provided considerable freedom to her students and this is a sign of the teacher taking on the role of facilitator, guide, mentor, and role model and she provides room for the students to 'find their own place in the classroom'.

In her discussion of the affinity between standards-based teaching and authentic academic achievement Stripling (1999) offers the following table:

Standards-Based teaching	Authentic Academic Achievement
1. Construction of meaning by students, not delivery of meaning by teachers	1. Construction of knowledge: developing the student's own ideas rather than indulging in simple reproducing of facts and ideas from others
2. In-depth, rather than superficial and broad, approach to curriculum and learning experiences	2. Disciplined inquiry: following the process of inquiry to construct in-depth understanding, based on prior knowledge, then communicating the new understanding
3. Emphasis on the application to real life situations in designing learning activities and assessment instruments	3. Value beyond the school: each student's knowledge and abilities have value beyond simply demonstrating competence at schoolwork; the product has value for others

Figure 1. Criteria for Authentic Learning

Source: Adapted from Stripling, B. (1999).

The picture (generated by Figure 1.) is one of a teacher who steps back from 'sage' to 'guide' and steps forward from 'knowing the class' to 'knowing each student'. This is difficult but essential!

Teacher control, no matter how well intentioned, does not provide a platform for the development of independent thinking or ownership by the students, of the processes of learning.

Likewise, teachers who do not know their students are not able to judge their construction process, nor are they able to make comprehensive judgments about what is a real life situation for each student.

Ainsworth and Christinson (1998) suggest that allowing students to generate their own rubrics achieves an answer to student ownership of learning and the assessment of that learning. They provide teachers with a five-step process. Teachers select focus questions identifying the big ideas to be learned and design learning activities and a performance task that allow all students to show what they are learning.

Teachers guide students as they create a task-specific rubric with objectives that are understandable to everyone.

- Students use the rubric to evaluate their own and their peers' work;

- Teachers review the student evaluations and determine the final grades;

- Students reflect on their performance with the help of the evaluations.

Developing a rubric is a reflective process that extends the experience and the knowledge gained beyond the parameters of traditional learning.

> **By actively participating in the assessment of their own progress, students become motivated, independent learners.**

And as their understanding of quality work grows, so does their level of personal responsibility. Construction of a rubric will facilitate a holistic understanding of issues and lead to a deeper understanding of the subject matter and the processes of construction.

Knowledge that has deep meaning provides the platform from which a learner is able to judge objectively their own work as well as that of others.

The rubric provides just one way to enable learners to take control of their learning. Whatever the approach that is used giving learners greater control over their learning and how that learning will be judged and by whom it will be judged must be a positive thing.

The role of audience

How important is the audience in obtaining both quality in the learning and quality feedback on that learning? It is worth pondering over your colleague's choice of audience and considering the impact that might have on student motivation, and the quality of the feedback to the students.

It could be argued that consideration of audience is often considered as an after-thought, if considered at all.

> **The more appropriate, or 'authentic' the audience, the better the fit between performance and feedback.**

If the teacher alone is the audience the students are only occasionally provided with an expert, and even then, with only one expert.

Of course it is unrealistic to expect that an expert audience can be provided for every piece of student assessment. Nevertheless, it should be considered in the design of the learning.

> **One way of putting learners in touch with an authentic audience is to make use of electronic tools and techniques.**

One such technique is the WebQuests. (Dodge: 2001; Hanson: 2001; and March: 1998). Hanson argues that WebQuest design incorporates the principles of authentic assessment; develops a set of realistic roles for the 'players'; and provides real world feedback. In addition Hanson notes the role that scaffolding plays in the WebQuest to enhance learning.

She identifies the following scaffolds:

- Reception scaffolds provide guidance in learning from a given resource that the students may not have seen before. Examples are tips on how to conduct interviews, online glossaries and dictionaries.

- Transformation scaffolds provide explicit help on transforming what is read into some new form. They can include help with brainstorming, finding patterns, comparing and contrasting and decision-making.

- Production aspects can be scaffolded by providing students with templates prompted writing guides, and multimedia elements.

- Rubrics to focus the process in terms of teamwork and evaluation.

Assessment and workload issues

Teachers often become buried in assessment and if this impacts on their ability to find time for research and reflection, planning and collegiality, it will be detrimental to teacher practice.

The evidence of over-assessment and inefficient assessment can be seen in many staff rooms where teachers are literally buried behind piles of scripts awaiting marking. That is one of the reasons why authentic assessment may be unpopular and why examinations, and summative assessment in general are so popular - even though they may not work!

This chapter may seem to encourage teachers to spend more time on assessment and it does! But what is being encouraged is greater integration of assessment with learning.

> *This means that teachers are able to deal with assessment throughout learning rather than just after the event.*

As far as possible teachers should share the assessment load and this can be achieved in many ways. Teachers can collaborate as assessors. This is particularly powerful when teachers with different specialities work together.

Students can share the assessment workload. This can be achieved by their involvement in designing the assessment form and specifics. It can be realised by facilitating self-assessment and peer assessment of individual and group work. Group assessment can be a powerful form of peer assessment and it has the added bonus that it results in fewer pieces of assessment!

> *Dealing with the challenge of the quantity of assessment on the desk will bring a reflective rigour to teaching that will result in benefits to the learners as well as to the teachers.*

Conclusion

The intention of this chapter was to raise awareness and to provoke debate about some issues to do with assessing learning. Students may regard assessment as isolated from the learning. Teachers may regard assessment as a chore.

> **Quality assessment takes time to create and is enhanced by the learner's involvement.**

Time invested in creating authentic assessment, is likely to mean that students will gain from it and perhaps even enjoy it. When learners are given ownership of their assessment the result is a lower pile of marking on the teacher's desk.

So what advice will you give your colleague?

References

Ainsworth, L. & Christinson, J. (1998). Student generated rubrics: An assessment model to help all students succeed. Palo Alto, CA: Dale Seymour Publications.

ATLC. (1995). Students' bill of information rights. http://www.atlc.ca/AboutATLC/studrigh.htm

Baron, J. B. and Wolf, D. P. (eds.). (1996). *Performance-based student assessment: Challenges and possibilities.* Chicago, IL: University of Chicago Press.

Belanoff, P. and Dickson, M., (eds.). (1991). *Portfolios: process and product.* Portsmouth, NH: Boynton/Cook.

Biggs, J. (1995). Assessing for learning: Some dimensions underlying new approaches to educational assessment. *The Alberta Journal of Educational Research,* 41(1): 1-17.

Bloom, B. (1956) Taxonomy of educational objectives: The cognitive domain. London: Longman.

Callison, D. (1994). The potential for portfolio assessment. In Kuhlthau, C.C. (ed.). *Assessment and the school library media center.* Englewood, Colo.: Libraries Unlimited: 121-130.

Callison, D. (1994a). Expanding the evaluation role in the critical-thinking curriculum. In Kuhlthau, C.C. (ed.). *Assessment and the school library media center.* Englewood, Colo.: Libraries Unlimited: 43-57.

Chicago Board of Education. (2000). Steps in developing a scoring rubric, http://intranet.cps.k12.il.us/Assessments/Ideas_and_Rubrics/Create_Rubric/create_rubric.html

De Bono, E. (1987). Six thinking hats. London: Penguin Books.

Diez, M.E. and Moon, C.J. (1992). What do we want students to know? *Educational Leadership*, 49 (8): 22-23.Dodge, B. (2001). FOUS: Five rules for writing a great WebQuest. *Learning & Leading with Technology*. www.iste.org/L&L/archive/vol28/no8/featuredarticle/dodge/index.html

Gardner, H. (1983). Frames of mind. NY: Basic Books.

Hanson, K. (2001). Beyond read and recall: An introduction to web-based learning using WebQuests. Paper presented at: Learning for a successful tomorrow: A workshop. CEO Wagga Wagga: 27-28 July.

Henri, J. (1996). Students on the Net: Enhancing learning through authentic assessment. In Hay, L. and Henri, J. (eds.). *A meeting of the minds: ITEC virtual conference '96 proceedings*. Belconnen, ACT: ASLA: 109-111.

Henri, J. (1999). Real teachers do assessment. In, Hay, L. and Henri, J. (eds.) The net effect. London: Scarecrow Press. 235-241.

Information Power: Building partnerships for learning. (1998) Chicago, ILL: American Library Association and Association for Educational Communications and Technology. See: The nine information literacy standards for student learning. At http://www.ala.org/aasl/ip_nine.html

Johnston, P., Guice, S., Baker, K., Malone, J. and Michelson, N. (1995). Assessment of teaching and learning in literature-based classrooms. *Teaching and Teacher Education*, 11(4): 359-371.

Kuhlthau, C.C. (1983). The library research process: Case studies and interventions with high school seniors in advanced placement English classes using Kelly's Theory of Constructs. Ed.D. Dissertation. Rutgers University.

Kuhlthau, C.C. (1993). Seeking meaning. Norwood, NJ: Ablex.

Lidz, C.S. (1995). Dynamic assessment and the legacy of L.S. Vygotsky. *School Psychology International*, 16: 143-153.

Lupton, P. (1996). Assessing students' work from the Net: an impossible dream? In Hay, L. and Henri, J. (eds.) *A meeting of the minds: ITEC virtual conference '96 proceedings*. Belconnen, ACT: ASLA: 112-114.

McGregor, J.H. (1993). Cognitive processes and the use of information. PhD Florida State University.

March, T. (1998). Why WebQuests? An introduction. http://www.ozline.com/webquests/intro.html

Norris, S.P. and Ennis, R.H. (1989). *Evaluating critical chinking*. Pacific Grove, CA: Critical Learning Books & Software.

O'Connell, J. and Henri, J. (1997). Information literacy: Teacher's perspectives of the information process. Paper presented at IASL-ATLC conference. Vancouver, July 8.

OSLA (1998) Information Studies: Kindergarten to Grade 12 curriculum for schools and school library information centres. http://www.accessola.org/action/positions/info_studies/html /preface.html

Perrone, V, (ed.). (1991). *Expanding student assessment*. Alexandria, Virginia: Association for Supervision and Curriculum Development.

Phye, G, (ed.). (1997). *Handbook of classroom assessment: learning, achievement, and adjustment*. San Diego: Academic Press.

Pitts, J. M. (1994). Personal understandings and mental models of information. PhD. Florida State University.

Popham, W. J. (1995). *Classroom assessment: what teachers need to know*. Boston: Allyn and Bacon.

Prince Edward Island, Department of Education. (1998) Building information literacy. http://www.edu.pe.ca/bil/

Spandel, V., and Stiggins R. J. (1997). *Creating writers: Linking assessment and writing instruction* (revised edition). White Plains, NY: Addison-Wesley Longman.

Stiggins, R. J. (1997). *Student-centered classroom assessment.* 2nd (ed.) Upper Saddle River, N.J.: Merrill.

Stiggins, R. J. (2001) Student-involved classroom assessment, 3rd Edition. Columbus, OH: Merrill.

Stripling, B. (1994). 'Assessment of student performance: the fourth step in the instructional design process.' In Kuhlthau, C.C. (ed.). *Assessment and the school library media center.* Englewood, Colo.: Libraries Unlimited: 77-93.

Stripling, B. (1999). Expectations for achievement and performance: Assessing student skills. NASSP Bulletin. March : 44-50.

University of Alberta, Faculty of Education. Alberta Initiative for school improvement. (2000). Authentic assessment. http://www.rockyview.ab.ca/cis/issues.htm

Webb, Noreen M. (1995). Group Collaboration in Assessment: Multiple Objectives, Processes, and Outcomes. *Educational Evaluation and Policy Analysis*, 17(2): 239-261.

Wiggins, G. (1993). *Assessing Student Performance.* San Francisco: Jossey-Bass.

Wiggins, Grant. (1989). A True Test: Toward More Authentic and Equitable Assessment. *Phi Delta Kappan,* (May): 703-713.

Wolf, D., J. Bixby, J. Glenn and H. Gardner, (eds.). (1991). *To use their minds well: investigating new forms of student assessment.* Washington, D.C.: American Educational Research Association.

Examples of Problem-based Tasks –
Lower School

Teachers from a wide variety of schools have contributed the following examples of problem-based tasks. We acknowledge and thank them for their willingness to share their ideas.

The emphasis in the following examples is on moving away from the concept of a topic, with students having only the opportunity to relate facts and figures, to that of a problem. The term "problem" has been used with the intention of presenting a task that provides the opportunity for the student to offer original thoughts and ideas after having researched the topic – with no single "right" answer.

In the following examples, the topic from which the problem is developed has been given as the starting point. Although by their very nature, problem-based tasks are open-ended, the unit can be contained and parameters or boundaries established by nominating in the criteria what specifically teachers want the students to do.

In each case, very clear criteria must be set in order for there to be no misunderstanding as to what is required, and in order for the students to know exactly what they have to do.

If appropriate, students will have more ownership and involvement in the task if they are given the opportunity of being involved in negotiating their own criteria.

Topic: **Frogs**
Problem: Whereabouts in the school grounds will we release our tadpoles when they have grown into frogs?

Topic: **Farms and farming**
Problem: If you could be a farmer when you grow up, what kind of farmer would you like to be?

Topic: **Circuses**
Concept: Circus performers are clever at entertaining people.
Problem: If you could be a **circus performer** when you grow up, which would you choose to be?

Topic: **Australian explorers**
Problem: If you were the **explorer** Burke, what would you have done differently?

Topic: **Famous Australians**
Problem: Nominate your choice for Australian of the Century Award.

Topic: **Australian States**
Problem: Choose the State of Australia where you would most like to live.

Topic: **Disasters**
Problem: Design an evacuation plan in the event of a (nominated disaster) for your local community.

Topic: **Families**
Problem: Compare your family to that of a kangaroo family.

Topic: **Middle Ages**
Problem: You are a serf living in small Medieval village. Write a diary of your daily life.

Topic: **Diet and nutrition**
Problem: Design a menu for a fortnight that will improve your own health and caters to your particular needs.

Problem: Design a menu for the Australian Soccer/Hockey/Rugby Union Team.

Problem: The School Canteen has been asked to provide only healthy food to the students. Design a menu they could offer.

Topic: **Birds/Reptiles/Fish/Animals**
Research 4 different species then choose one to recommend as a new addition to your local fauna reserve or zoo.

Topic: **Pets**
Problem: Choose the pet you think would be most suitable for your family/classroom.

Topic: **Inventions**
Problem: Choose a modern household utensil. Trace its history and predict what it might become in the future.

Topic: **Friendship**
Problem: What makes me a good friend?

Topic: **Sportsmanship**
Problem: What makes me a good sport?

Examples of Problem-Based Tasks –
Middle School

Teachers of The King's School, in collaboration with Megan Perry Head of Library and Information Services, and Debbie Leatheam Teacher librarian, designed the following problem-based tasks – tasks that provided the opportunity for students to create original thoughts and ideas.

A Famous Scientist
Advertising

These tasks are based on an acceptance of the need to scaffold and embed both information and computing skills within each assignment. Additionally, school-based policies underpin the **'whole school approach'** and lend weight and integrity to the process, which is based on a constantly evolving model.

In the chapter of this book entitled *Snapshots of Information Literacy,* Megan Perry explains the process that was devised at The King's School to facilitate the development of worthy and developmentally appropriate student assignments.

Each of the underlined words in the following tasks is a link to a site, or to material that provides additional scaffolding and support for the students.

Permission to share these examples
has kindly been given by:
Ms Megan Perry, Head of Information Services,
Ms D Leatheam, Teacher-librarian,
Mr T Rocks and Mr E Dobbin
The King's School,
Parramatta, New South Wales

A Famous Scientist - Year 7

Background Information: Science is a special method of finding out knowledge and solving problems. You have been studying this in class. Observation, experiment, measurement and testing ideas are all part of this method.

Not all scientists solve problems in the same way you have in class.
Some problems are simple and can be solved with a few experiments.
Other problems are much harder to solve.
Some scientific discoveries are accidental.
Some scientific discoveries start off as accidents.
Some scientific discoveries come from people's 'thoughts'.

The task: Here are two lists of famous scientists. Choose one scientist from each list.

Before 1900	After 1900
Nicholas Copernicus (1473)	Barbara McClintock (1902)
Galileo Galilei (1564)	Robert Oppenheimer (1904)
Isaac Newton (1642)	Sir John Cornforth (1917)
Charles Darwin (1809)	Rosalind Franklin (1920)
Edmond Halley (1656)	Carl Sagan (1934)
Benjamin Franklin (1706)	Stephen Hawking (1942)
Louis Pasteur (1822)	Robert Ballard (1942)
Pierre Curie (1809)	Francis Crick (1916)
Sir MacFarlane Burnett (1899)	Christiaan Barnard (1922)
	Walter Massey (1938)

Create a booklet to describe the lives of your chosen scientists, following the plan outlined below.

Use **A4 size** pages, one for each item. Include a bibliography sheet.

☐	Create a **Title page**. Give the name of the two scientists you intend to review, and your name, as the author of the work. (Date and name of publisher also)
☐	Write the **birth notices** for your scientists, as they would appear in the 'newspaper' of the day. Make them as authentic as possible....
☐	Write a brief **description** of a day in the life of each of your scientists, including some information about the society in which they lived. (150 words each) Write one for each scientist.
☐	Include a **'photograph'** of the scientist you chose from after 1900. Draw or cut a picture from a magazine of what you think he/ she may have looked like, and write a caption to explain what is happening in the photo at that moment. *No photocopies accepted - not even of the 'real' scientist.*
☐	Prepare a **table of facts** for each of the scientists you have chosen that outlines their achievements and discoveries.
☐	Using the information about the scientists you have gathered in your table, describe and compare of the **processes** of experimenting, observing, measuring and recording, and finding information that each of your scientists has experienced.
☐	Sketch the tombstone of your after 1900 scientist as it might appear in the future in the local cemetery. In particular, what would the epitaph say?

Advertising - Year 8

Aims: ☐ To develop an understanding of the role and purpose of advertising in 2000.

☐ To understand the methods used to effectively advertise a product.

☐ To investigate the power of online advertising and marketing.

☐ To assess the information provided on an Internet site.

Task: ☐ Working in pairs, complete the following tasks.

☐ *Case Study* - choose an **existing product** and answer the following questions.

In **3 - 4 sentences**, describe the nature of your product. How has this product been promoted? To whom? (Consider the targeted audience in your answer). Suggest **4 effective media** that this company has chosen to promote their product. Explain why you think it is effective/ineffective promotion. What changes would you have made to one of these advertisements, if you had the opportunity? Why?

☐ You are an *advertising agency* - a team of two.

Create a **complete portfolio** to present to your clients for a product of your choice. Include the following details, and two extra details of your choice.

Name of your agency	Product presented	Advertising campaign plan
Slogan	Logo	3 suggestions for effective promotion/ marketing
plus....2 visual ideas of your own		

Online shopping -
List 10 different **types** of products that can be purchased online.
Search engine home pages all have lists, e.g.,Yahoo

Choose three different products, access them online and assess
the presentation of the site's information, using the questionnaire
handout *For guidance and printout.*

Accessing current articles:
Using either **Guidelines**, **World magazine bank** or the **online
newspapers** e.g., *Australian Financial Review*, search for and
access an article about the current advertising environment. Write
a full bibliographic reference for the article, and in a paragraph,
explain what it is about.

From the **periodical collection** held in the Library, in what **titles**
would you expect to find relevant articles about **aspects of the
advertising world**. List 4 titles.

Task requirements: A written response for all four parts.

Case Study - short written answers.
Present your own product as a *complete portfolio.*
Online shopping - print out, and fill in the **chart**.
Bibliography details, title list and *current article* summary.

The following examples of problem-centred tasks, based on the concept of scenarios, were designed for a Middle School Science class, and are an example of how tasks requiring an original response might be presented to the students.

The tasks were given out to students in personally addressed envelopes, and each task was individually addressed to the student.

The teacher chose which students received each task – dependent upon ability level, perceived interest level, etc.

Tasks include:
Albatross **Insurance** investigation
LAPD Internal Memo
Loch Ness Monster – Fact or fiction
Debunking **Unexplained Mysteries** Bureau
The curse of **Tutankhamen**
Vampires – Fact, fiction or folklore
A **Viking's** Dream

The tasks were designed by:
Roberta Longhurst
in collaboration with teacher librarians:
Mary-Ann Salisbury and **Deborah Jones**
Runcorn State High School
Queensland

Permission to include these examples
has kindly been granted by
Education Queensland

Albatross Insurance

Memo

To: Trent

From: Managing Director

Date: 12/04/02

Re: Market Research

Assignment

As an employee of Albatross Insurance, you will be well aware that we dare to go where no other insurance company has gone before. Now that we have financially recovered from our Titanic, Heidelberg and S.O.C.O.G. debacle, we feel in a secure enough position to venture further field again.

We have found an untouched market located between the Florida coast of the U.S.A., Bermuda and Puerto Rico. For some reason, inhabitants have had previous problems securing insurance for their planes and boats.

We need you Trent, to investigate this area. Figure out whether there are any reasons as to why insurance is nonexistent at this point in time. If there are areas of concern, research and find out any plausible explanations.

We don't want to declare bankruptcy again so please be thorough.

L.A.P.D. Internal Memorandum

Attention: Detective Courtney

From: Lieutenant Cenitalbefaw

Date: 12/04/02

Re: Insurance Payout Investigation

Case:

Courtney, we need you to reinvestigate the death of Cindy Ash as the bubble headed state coroner passed judgment that her death was not suspicious.

Yeah right! A body B.B.Q'd to cinders 'cept for arms and legs, found slap bang in her favourite Jason recliner nothin' else burnt, ain't suspicious? We may as well say her money-hungry third husband works part time for the salvos!

I want to nail that toe rag and you're going to do it Detective Courtney. Autopsy notes are useless, 'cept for no known propellants found at the crime scene. But ... surprise, surprise - lover boy 3 is a fireman, so that means nothin'. You gotta make this stick, so be real careful.

We're gonna go to court and make sure he don't get no joy from his Missus' insurance payout!

Loch Ness Monster - Fact or Fiction

'Och aye Bradley , Nessie's there. I've lived all my life since I was a wee lad. I canna guarantee you'll see her, but she's there!'

Bradley looked at his Uncle fondly. He knew Uncle Angus was passionate about his Nessie but so far Bradley had found no absolute proof to substantiate the extraordinary claim.

'But Uncle, I have seen Nessie already, hundreds of them. There is a shop down the road called Nessie's Knick-knacks. They've got Nessie nutcrackers, Nessie…………

'You cheeky little…' Angus raised a ferociously reprimanding red eyebrow, "I'll have you know Monks – religious men – saw Nessie 500 hundred years ago, before any damn tourist set foot in the place. Are you calling them liars as well?"

Bradley felt bad about upsetting Uncle Angus. The only way to make things better was to investigate these sightings and to find out whether there was any conceivable way that a monster could really exist.

And then if an apology were required, Bradley would give it. Uncle Angus would dish up haggis for every meal if he thought himself hard done by.

PRIVATE AND CONFIDENTIAL

**Debunking
Unexplained Mysteries
Bureau**

Memo

To: Agent William

From: Chief

Date: 12/04/02

Re: Destination – Caribbean Island off Haiti

Background Information:
In 1962, Clairvius Narcisse died of a supposed heart attack. A traditional funeral followed with the body being interned in a three metre deep plot. Sixteen years later his sister found him walking around in a dazed state in the local village. Positive identification of this individual confirmed he was indeed, the living dead. This area is deeply entrenched in Voodoo culture where high priests and priestess supposedly conjure up the dead by the use of cantations, lotions and potions and secret ceremonies.

Assignment:
As our DUMB employee of the month William, we want you to travel to Haiti (make sure you use your frequent flyers) and research what is really going on. How do they make zombies and more importantly why? Submit a report on your return.

Footnote:
Make sure you keep all meal receipts.

The Curse of Tutankhamen

And the hieroglyphics written on the wall of the boy king's tomb read –

Death will come to those who disturb the sleep of the pharaohs

The guide whispered in an awestruck voice, as if he did not wish to insult the long dead inhabitant of the dusty dark tomb.
"What a load of beetle dung!" bellowed the overweight American man.
"Bet you those fancy drawings aren't as old as my underpants. Anything for the Yankee tourist dollar, hey Abdul? Ten bucks for a bumpy camel ride, ten bucks to crawl through dusty passageways, $400 for Luxor Lodge, $100 to see some cruddy drawings in a room you couldn't swing a mummified cat in. Curses for purses.
Are you listening to me Upinder?
I'm not happy! I'm not happy at all!"

"Good grief," thought Upinder, "this obnoxious fat slimy toad is my boss, and if he's not happy, I'm out of a job."

"It's up to you, Upinder. I want you to debunk this bally-hoo nonsense. I want a report, and I want it yesterday. Before I spend another cent in this hellhole I want you to earn your keep as my researcher, and find out if there is anything to these curses. I want facts, and I want èm now!"

"Great!" grumbled Upinder, "Luxor Library here I come"

A thick layer of snow that shone blue-white in the frosty moonlight blanketed the Transylvanian forest. Needle sharp fangs plunged again and again into the alabaster flesh. Crimson rivulets of blood trickled down the blue white skin and dripped, the snow melting on contact as if it was acid.

It's inhuman hunger temporarily sated, the fanged creature licked its mouth meticulously, savouring the last salty drops. Life force spent, the victim lay in a crumpled heap, a look of naked terror reflected in lifeless eyes.

Unseemly laughter and music floated up through the trees. Golden light spilled out of the cottage windows pinpointing the location of more naive victims. The ancient clawing hunger returning, the evil beast narrowed soulless eyes and soundlessly flew on blackened wings.

Another victim perhaps, before the fingers of dawn commanded its retreat to the bowels of the earth below.

Tahlia - find out whether this is Fact, Fiction or Folklore

A Viking's Dream

Shafeen surveyed his village with pride. Three massive dragon ships were nearing completion and the storage huts were brimming with winter provisions, harvested from the previous bountiful summer. Ironmongers tempered the broad swords and axes to razor sharp edge. In two more moons they would leave. Before the icepacks anchored them to home for the long Nordic winter, Shafeen and his men would set sail for the southern lands. He grinned mercilessly at the thought of the carnage and pilling in the days to come.

His warriors would fight without fear, confident that death in the battlefield would give them admittance to Valhalla. A lifetime of drinking and wenching in the beautiful Valhyries guaranteed.

Shafeen's gaze drifted upwards into the midnight blue sky. Shimmering lights danced across the heavens, entrance to the great hall of Valhalla.

"It won't be long until my men and I are up there," thought Shafeen. "Victorious and immortal in death, we will be invisible."
                    But were they?

Examples of Problem-Based Tasks – Upper School

The following examples of problem-based tasks, providing opportunities for students to create original responses, are based on the concept of point-of-view, and were designed for an
Upper School Geography unit
with particular students in mind.

The tasks were devised by:
Phillipa Grobler
In collaboration with teacher librarians:
Mary-Ann Salisbury and **Deborah Jones**
and with kind permission of the Principal,
Mr John Hodgkinson,
to share this work.

Runcorn State High School
Queensland.

Permission has kindly been given by
Education Queensland
to include these examples.

Students were asked to respond to the following tasks
set as seminar presentations by developing an
original solution to the problem presented:

Seminar Response

**You have been requested to write a recommendation,
which suggests a solution to each of the major
world environment problems discussed during the
World Environment Conference 2002.**

- Listen carefully to each presentation

- Write some notes to help you to consider the main
  aspects of the problem and the main interest groups
  whose needs must be considered.

- Present a solution or a recommendation, which will
  solve the environmental problem, will work and will
  satisfy all the interest groups.

- Explain your solution in about 200 words.

- Write your solution at the end of each presentation so
  you don't forget the information you need to consider.

WORLD ENVIRONMENT CONFERENCE 2002

Memo

To: Ashley, Andrew, Adam, Jay
From: Theodore Green
Date: Semester 1, 2002
Re: Seminar Presentation

You and your team have been invited to give a presentation at the upcoming world environment seminar 2002. Delegates from all over the world will be present to learn, discuss and make decisions about major issues that will impact on the environment so heavily that they will or could affect human existence on earth.

The 1990's were the warmest decade for the past thousand years and with the withdrawal of the United States from the Kyoto agreement **global warming** has become an important issue.

Each member of the team will present information from a different perspective. For instance global warming can be seen from an environmental point of view or government, industry or consumer viewpoints. You need to decide on these viewpoints after you have done some initial research. This will affect each person's presentation of the "facts" and make each person's seminar unique.

Delegates (your classmates) will listen to your presentation and be required to write a paper to propose a solution to the problem you present.

WORLD ENVIRONMENT
CONFERENCE 2002

Memo

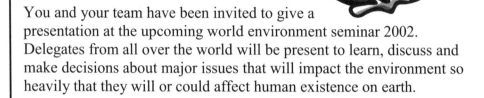

To: Aaron, Aaron, Ryan, Meekaeel
From: Theodore Green
Date: Semester 1, 2002
Re: Seminar Presentation

You and your team have been invited to give a
presentation at the upcoming world environment seminar 2002.
Delegates from all over the world will be present to learn, discuss and
make decisions about major issues that will impact the environment so
heavily that they will or could affect human existence on earth.

The world has been appalled by the spectre of **foot and mouth disease**
in the United Kingdom recently – the distress of farmers, the burning
piles of cattle carcasses, the quarantine and the job of the army and vets
to diagnose and deal with this disease. This disease is likely to impact
on the natural environment and has implications also for other aspects
of the human environment.

Each member of your team will present information from
a different perspective on this topic. For instance, you
can discuss any of the viewpoints above or that of
environmentalists or the tourism industry. You need to
decide on these viewpoints after you have done some
research. This will affect each person's presentation of the "facts" and
make each person's seminar unique.

Delegates (your classmates) will listen to your presentation and
be required to write a paper to propose a solution to the problem
you present.

WORLD ENVIRONMENT CONFERENCE 2002

Memo

To: Tim, Joel, Andrew, Antony
From: Theodore Green
Date: Semester 1, 2002
Re: Seminar Presentation

You and your team have been invited to give a presentation at the upcoming world environment seminar 2002. Delegates from all over the world will be present to learn, discuss and make decisions about major issues that will impact the environment so heavily that they will or could affect human existence on earth.

Salinity is costing Australia $270 million and affects approximately 2.5 million hectares. As such it is not just an agricultural problem but a national problem, which will affect us all now, and in the future. It will cost us much more the longer we leave the problem untreated.

Each member of the team will present information from a different perspective. For instance salinity can be seen from an environmental point of view or government, farming or small town viewpoints. You need to decide on these viewpoints after you have done some initial research. This will affect each person's presentation of the "facts" and make each person's seminar unique.

Delegates - (your classmates) will listen to your presentation and be required to write a paper to propose a solution to the problem you present.

WORLD ENVIRONMENT
CONFERENCE 2002

Memo

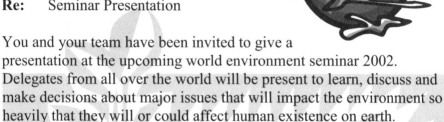

To: Brendon, Sasha, Peter, William
From: Theodore Green
Date: Semester 1, 2002
Re: Seminar Presentation

You and your team have been invited to give a
presentation at the upcoming world environment seminar 2002.
Delegates from all over the world will be present to learn, discuss and
make decisions about major issues that will impact the environment so
heavily that they will or could affect human existence on earth.

Burning rainforest in the Amazon affecting the climate; grasslands in
Australia where there used to be forest and burning forest in Indonesia
polluting the air in Indonesia, Malaysia and Singapore. **Deforestation** is
a major world environmental problem the effects of which we are
still uncertain.

Each member of the team will present information from a different
perspective. For instance deforestation can be seen from an
environmental point of view or government, farming or economic
viewpoints. You need to decide on these viewpoints after you have done
some initial research. This will affect each person's presentation of the
"facts" and make each person's seminar unique.

Delegates (your classmates) will listen to your presentation and
be required to write a paper to propose a solution to the problem
you present.

WORLD ENVIRONMENT CONFERENCE 2002

Memo

To: Suzanne, Jasmine, Matthew, Trent
From: Theodore Green
Date: Semester 1, 2002
Re: Seminar Presentation

You and your team have been invited to give a presentation at the upcoming world environment seminar 2002. Delegates from all over the world will be present to learn, discuss and make decisions about major issues that will impact the environment so heavily that they will or could affect human existence on earth.

Over fishing and the **depletion of fish stocks** is an issue of rising concern. Driftnet fishing methods and pollution of the ocean do not make this issue any easier to deal with. Past over fishing has pushed whale stocks to the brink of extinction.

Each member of the team will present information from a different perspective. For instance, fishery issues can be seen from an environmental point of view or government, fisherman or economic viewpoints. You need to decide on these viewpoints after you have done some initial research. This will affect each person's presentation of the "facts" and make each person's seminar unique.

Delegates (your classmates) will listen to your presentation and be required to write a paper to propose a solution to the problem you present.

Index